New Directions in Theology Today

VOLUME IV
The Church

New Directions in Theology Today
WILLIAM HORDERN, GENERAL EDITOR

VOL. I INTRODUCTION
BY WILLIAM HORDERN

VOL. II HISTORY AND HERMENEUTICS
BY CARL E. BRAATEN

VOL. III GOD AND SECULARITY
BY JOHN MACQUARRIE

VOL. IV THE CHURCH
BY COLIN W. WILLIAMS

VOL. V CHRISTIAN LIFE
BY PAUL HESSERT

VOL. VI MAN: THE NEW HUMANISM
BY ROGER LINCOLN SHINN

VOL. VII CHRIST
BY ROBERT CLYDE JOHNSON

NEW DIRECTIONS IN THEOLOGY TODAY

Volume IV
The Church

BY
COLIN W. WILLIAMS

Lutterworth Press
London

First published 1969

COPYRIGHT © MCMLXVIII THE WESTMINSTER PRESS

7188 1389 8

PRINTED IN GREAT BRITAIN PHOTOLITHO
BY EBENEZER BAYLIS AND SON, LTD.
THE TRINITY PRESS, WORCESTER, AND LONDON

Editor's Foreword

Theology always has existed in some tension with the church. But there is considerable evidence that today the gulf is wider than ever before. To both pastors and laymen it often seems that contemporary theology is working in opposition to the concerns of the parish. They are disturbed to read in newspapers and popular journals about theologians who seem to have lightly cast aside the cornerstones of the faith and who argue that the parish is doomed. To the theologian the parish often appears to be a respectable club dedicated to erecting buildings, raising budgets, and avoiding controversial issues.

There is little active dialogue between the theologian and the church today. The fault for this lies with both parties, but the situation is becoming increasingly serious as the church moves into a new age. This series is dedicated to the task of bridging the present gulf.

One of the reasons for the gulf between theology and the church is that neither the busy pastor nor the concerned layman can keep up to date with an ever-expanding theological literature. Thus, the purpose of New Directions in Theology Today is to present concise summaries of the present scene in theology. The series is not for the lazy pastor, nor for the layman who is beginning his theological education. Rather, these volumes are especially prepared for the busy pastor who is concerned with keeping abreast of modern theology and for the layman who, having been initiated into theology, is reading for further study, particularly to find out what contemporary Christian thinkers are saying.

The series is not written with the assumption that only professional theologians have something to say, but is offered in the hope that it will stimulate pastors and laymen to enter into the theological dialogue, and with the conviction that a vital theology for our time must be the work of the church as a whole.

WILLIAM HORDERN

Contents

CHAPTER I

The Radical Shift in Focus

At the First Assembly of the World Council of Churches held in 1948 in Amsterdam, Father Georges Florovsky insisted that the doctrine of the church (ecclesiology) had scarcely passed its pretheological phase. Christology had been battled out in the first five centuries and formulated in the creeds and in the statements of the councils. While the person of Christ (Christology) dominated early theological discussions, the work of Christ (atonement) received its full attention in the Middle Ages, and the spotlight of attention was turned on the Sacraments in the late Middle Age and Reformation periods. But little direct theological attention was ever given to the church itself—probably because it was taken for granted.

Not even with the radical divisions of the church in Europe and the New World did major attention turn to ecclesiology. In Europe there was continuing acquiescence in state churches through the post-Reformation stages of Christendom, for it was assumed that an established church and a divinely ordered state were the two inseparable arms of God's one government of the world. This meant that the question of the church scarcely arose. It was assumed that the role of the church was obvious.

In the New World the struggles to adapt church institutions to new environments at first absorbed such theological energies as were available into the practical tasks of mission. Then a strong attitude developed among the cultural majority that the less thought there was of "church" and the more there was of "kingdom," the more healthy the Christian cause would be in its attempt to build the Kingdom of God in America. The ethnic minorities meantime tended to use their separate church identity as a protection against the threatening world of the majority. In neither of these attitudes did the theological question of the church become urgent.

The emergence of the church as a theological problem occurred in the mission fields—primarily the mission fields of Asia and Africa, where the separations between the various "missions" from the Old World revealed their absurdity as divided churches were planted in the strange soil of the old religions. The missionaries sensed the absurdity very quickly. Knowing there should be only one mission because there is only one Lord, they began to question Scripture and tradition to find why there were many churches and whether the many could again become one.

Out of this pressure from the mission field (and out of the same question arising from the mission field of the universities in the West, where the Student Christian Movement was quickly giving its answer from Scripture in its motto *Ut omnes unum sint*) arose the main impulse to the modern ecumenical movement. The movement was toward the vision of the unity of the church for the sake of the unity of the mission.

Inevitably then, ecclesiology was brought into the theological spotlight by the rise of the ecumenical movement.

As churches were drawn out of their centuries of isolation, they had to explain themselves to one another. Discovering their strangeness one to the other, they were forced to probe their own self-understanding; and, inspired by a vision of a unity that transcends their separate traditions, they began to search together for the tradition behind the traditions—the church behind the churches.

So it was that *self-conscious ecclesiology* became the hallmark of the early stage of the ecumenical movement, with Faith and Order, which gave its time to the probing of the question, becoming the aristocrat of the ecumenical order. But as the churches set out on the task of finding their oneness in Christ, it quickly became clear that this ecclesiological game was far from simple. It was at the First Assembly of the World Council of Churches that Father Florovsky issued his warning to the delegates. He reminded the delegates that Faith and Order had so far only explored some of the rough dimensions of the field. The "pretheological phase" was scarcely over.

All that could be done at Amsterdam, therefore, was to parade a series of witnesses to the speakers' platform to illustrate the conflicting viewpoints that were emerging in this early stage of the debate. One of the speakers, the Anglo-Catholic Bishop Gregg of Ireland, sought to define the church in terms of its "givenness" as the body of Christ in history, stressing the visible continuities of its life in ministry, creeds, Sacraments, and fellowship. But on the other side, Karl Barth insisted on the humanly uncontrollable "event" character of the church. It occurs as a gift of the Spirit where the Word evokes faith. Any visible continuities in the life of the church are removed from human institutional control.

These were but the most obvious poles of a complicated

debate which made Florovsky's warning an apparent truth. And since that time ecclesiology has remained at the center of the ecumenical theological spotlight. The unfolding story, however, contains a major surprise. It begins (we have noted) with *self-conscious ecclesiology*—inevitably the attempt was made to solve the problem of the churches by a *direct* attack on the doctrine of the church. But now it has reached the point where something of a consensus seems to be emerging—that the question of the church can be solved only when we first go beyond the church and ask the question of God's mission in the world. For the church is not an end in itself; it is the servant of the mission of God in the world, and for that reason the ecclesiological problem can be answered only *indirectly*.

To oversimplify, we can sketch the ecumenical ecclesiological story into the framework of the three periods marked by the assemblies of the World Council of Churches.

In the *first period* (from Amsterdam 1948 to Evanston 1954), the search for a common ecclesiology explored the "continuities" that lie behind our divisions. It can be called *a period of high-church rediscovery,* but not in the rather institutional Anglo-Catholic sense suggested by Bishop Gregg at Amsterdam. It was, rather, that the rich givenness of the corporate life of the covenant community was explored in the Biblical records and in the various traditions. Paul Minear's book *Images of the Church in the New Testament*[1] represents the rich fruit of the Biblical study of this period. In the New Testament imagery Minear discovered over a hundred terms for the church. At the same time historical studies were exploring fathers, Reformers, and the major theologians to search for their controlling visions of the continuing life of the church in history. The hope behind the research was clear. It was a search for the given unity of the church of Jesus Christ in the tradition behind the traditions, in the given fellowship that under-lies our broken communities. It was a search for the church as the continuing gift of Christ within the discontinuities of our divided histories.

In the *second period* (from Evanston 1954 to New Delhi 1961), a change in emphasis already begins to be discerni-ble. A suspicion began to grow that the inward-looking character of this ecclesiological search could be self-defeat-ing. Was it, perhaps, too "Christendom" conscious—too much dominated by the assumption that the church is to be found by looking within the churches? The result of this suspicion was the emphasis that *"mission" must be added as an essential mark of the church.* In looking for the true unity of the church we must look not only for visible con-tinuities (such as Word and Sacraments). We must look also for the event of obedience to the mission of Christ. Unity is given us not just in the historical continuities; it is a gift that is received only as we obey the one call to mission.

Here Barth's event emphasis can be seen to have re-entered. The church occurs, the emphasis was, in the event of faith and obedience. And with this the radical shift from the attempt to solve the problem of ecclesiology di-rectly was under way. In this stage, however, the shift seemed relatively modest. It was hoped that by reestablish-ing mission as the mark of the church which the Christen-dom churches had forgotten (including the Reformation churches), the true proportions of ecclesiology could be restored. In the period of Christendom when national churches acquiesced easily in their separations and (at their best) asked only whether the Word was being truly preached and the Sacraments duly administered, the mis-sion imperative to go in obedience to Christ to the ends of the earth and to draw all creation into one in him had been lost. It was even suggested that this apostolic command was completed in the apostolic period. The churches, as a result, had become virtual prisoners in the separate cultural life of their nations. But now, by adding obedience in mission to Word and Sacraments (and sometimes ministry) as the true marks of the church, it was felt that we should be abe to discern the way to the unity that is God's will and gift for us.

But in the *third period* (New Delhi 1961 to Uppsala 1968), the shift begins to appear in more radical form—in the very period when the ecumenical movement becomes less a Protestant movement and the Roman Catholic Church becomes deeply involved in the ecclesiological discussions, both through an incredible volume of work by her theologians and through the remarkable events of the Vatican Council, where ecclesiology was the dominant issue.

In this period we begin to hear that it is not enough to attempt to solve the problem of ecclesiology by adding "mission" to the classical "marks of the church." What is required is to move ecclesiology out of the center of theological concern, for as soon as ecclesiology becomes central it is falsified. The way to a true ecclesiology must be indirect, for the church is meant to be not an end in itself but the servant of God's mission to the world.

This emphasis became a hallmark of the World Council of Churches' study on "The Missionary Structure of the Congregation," as two quotes from its report *The Church for Others*[2] will make evident.

The Church exists for the world. It is called to the service of mankind, of the world. This is not election to privilege but to serving engagement. The Church lives in order that the world may know its true being. It is *pars pro toto;* it is the first fruits of the new creation. But its centre lies outside itself; it must live "ex-centredly." It has to seek out those situations in the world that call for loving responsibility and there it must announce and point to *shalom.* This ex-centric position of the Church implies that we must stop thinking from the inside towards the outside.[3]

And the second quotation:

The church is that part of the world where God's concern is recognized and celebrated. The church must be understood in its world-relation as an expression of God's will that all men be saved (I Tim. 2:3). This affirms its existence for all men (pro-existence). In terms of God's concern for the world, the church is a segment of the world, a *postscript,* that is, added to the world for the purpose of pointing to and celebrating both Christ's presence and God's ultimate redemption of the whole world.[4]

Lest it be thought that this emphasis simply represents the conquest of one World Council of Churches study by the forces of the left—an Anabaptist bid for an ecumenical take-over—it must be pointed out that the same emphasis emerged among some of the Roman Catholic theologians, and is clearly represented, too, in the work of an Orthodox theologian, Father Alexander Schmemann.[5]

Take, for example, the thesis set forward by the Roman Catholic theologian Hans Urs von Balthasar in his book *A Theology of History.*[6] The church, he affirms, is the servant of God's purpose in and for history and, for that reason, must not look for history to be drawn into itself. God is working out his purpose in the evolution of history and in that evolution the church appears very late.[7] At that late stage God chooses Israel as an instrument of his evolutionary work and as a sign of his purpose for all the nations. "Ethiop or Israelite, what care I?" the Lord says. "God that brought you here from Egypt is the God that brought the Philistines from Caphtor, brought the Syrians from Kir!" (Amos 9:7.) But Israel's life, and then through Christ the Christian church, is to be seen in God's total work in history as the point where the purpose of God for all history at last rises to visibility—a purpose broadening out into cosmic history as God's evolutionary purpose for his whole creation is realized in history. The church is called to be the place where that total purpose of God is given visibility. But that can happen, not by the church having a life separate from the world, but only as the church struggles in the world against the "powers" that stand in the way of God's purpose for the world. Because of that, Christ's struggle with his church to keep it available for his worldly purpose is in fact the "crucial battle" in history. "The struggle is the ultimate truth of history. It is the Lord's wrestling as a lover with his bride, the church."[8]

In this quotation, however, we are introduced to an important difference in emphasis among those who share this shift to the view that the church can be understood only indirectly within its servant task on behalf of God's mission to the world. For Balthasar the church is called into being by God as *the* pivotal sign for history. It does not exist for itself. It is only God's servant in his total mission for the world. But it is precisely in its excentric life—its life-for-the-world—that the world is meant to discern its own destiny.

Compare with that the following from Hans Hoekendijk:

When one desires to speak about God's dealings with the world, the church can be mentioned only in passing and without strong emphasis. Ecclesiology cannot be more than a single paragraph from Christology (the *Messianic* dealings with the world) and a few sentences from eschatology (the Messianic dealings with the *World*). The church is only the church to the extent that she lets herself be used as a part of God's dealings with the oikoumene. For this reason she can only be "ecumenical," i.e., oriented toward the oikoumene—the whole world.[9]

Clearly Balthasar gives a far more pivotal role to the community of the church in God's mission to the world. The nature of the role is described in similar terms, with the church being the servant of God's struggle in and for the world against the powers that stand in the way of that purpose. But the way that role is carried out is described quite differently. Balthasar emphasizes the need for the church to become visible at the point of the struggle as the sign to the world of its own destiny. Hoekendijk emphasizes the need for the church to find the points in the world where Christ is carrying out his struggle, and to make that struggle visible. For him, therefore, the emphasis is on the excentric character of the church. It must be fading into the background, pointing away from itself to Christ's humanizing work. For Balthasar, the emphasis is on the representative role of the church. It becomes visible in its excentric struggle for the world—itself the sign of Christ's humanizing work.

It may well be that this difference within the agreement will turn out to be of great significance. But important though the difference may be, it must not hide the crucial significance of the area of agreement in what we have spoken of as "the radical shift" in focus from the direct approach to ecclesiology to the indirect approach, with the church being seen as a postscript to the primary reality of God's mission to and for the world.

FROM THE CATEGORIES OF NATURE TO THE CATEGORIES OF HISTORY

There is another aspect to this radical shift which throws a great deal of light upon it, and which reveals other facets of its significance. There is considerable talk in contemporary theology of the way in which the categories of "nature," with the attempt to place reality in the ordered categories of structural metaphysics, are now giving way to the categories of "history," with the recognition that human reality must be understood in dynamic terms with the old secure ontological scaffolding removed.

To quote a typical statement of the change:

The being of God-in-himself, his nature and attributes, the nature of the church, the nature of man, the preexistent nature of Christ—all these conjectural topics which have drawn theology into a realm of either physical or metaphysical speculation remote from the habitation of living men should be abandoned. Not that the concerns they express should be evaded. Every doctrine which has existed in Christian theology embraces some historical intention. The task of an historical hermeneutic, an historical mode of interpretation, is to disengage the historical intention from the non-historical expression and to conserve and elaborate the intention.[10]

I have no doubt that this shift has occurred and must be welcomed.[11] Its importance for our approach to ecclesiology, however, is what concerns us here. And it is this shift, I believe, which lies behind the movement outlined in the three phases of ecumenical discussions on the church. The studies began within the traditional categories, but gradually moved across to the dynamic categories of history, with attention finally focusing on the role of the church as a historical institution within God's total historical purpose. The "objectifying" categories that describe in relatively static form the "nature" of the church were seen to be inadequate. The question became that of the role of the church in the actual situation where we are confronted by God's purpose in history.

As soon as we look at the present situation of the church in this way some important factors emerge:

1. We see that the church in our time is no longer in a position to lord it over the world in the old medieval sense, attempting to draw the whole of the culture under its "christianizing" influence. The church has lost its capacity to command and its power to control history institutionally. For that reason the servant role of which we have spoken is now the only one it can hope to fulfill.[12]

2. The church no longer can provide a stable center to culture—a controlling world view or value system to hold society together. But neither does our society look any longer for such a metaphysical or cultural or religious unity. This is at the very heart of the change from the old metaphysical attitude toward the historical attitude. There is no longer a dominant sense of need (at least in the West) for a controlling world view, and no longer a dominant sense of need for the church to provide a doctrinal "system" to give a stable framework for that world view. For that reason the flexible functional theology that is now replacing the older metaphysical forms of theology is more attuned to the mental attitude of our time.[13]

3. An increasing number of theologians are seeing this change from nature categories to history categories as itself the fruit of the Christian faith and as a healthy sign that the world is coming of age and growing out of its childhood need for the cultural scaffolding of *a* world view and the religious scaffolding of *an* established religious attitude (officially or unofficially). They see the exodus diaspora situation of the church as one that we should happily accept and as one that should free us to describe the church in functional terms which direct attention to the way of obedience to Christ as he works within these changes of our culture.

"Any conceptual system, however, which is static in character is essentially inadequate," writes Robert Adolfs.

The Church is to be envisaged first and foremost as *event* and not as an in essence already complete, realized entity which has, so to speak, appropriated all its assets. The Church is a continuing event that is being accomplished in history and *through* people. The being-called-together of people under Christ as the one Head (Eph. I.9.)—that in essence is the Church. But it is not something signed, sealed and delivered to us by God; rather is it—for all who belong to such a Church—*a continuing task*.[14]

This emphasis on the church as a project—a way of obedience which must be continually fashioned within the particular situation in history in the light of the ultimate purpose of God for history—opens the way to the radical change from the traditional forms of ecclesiology that we have inherited. It is not that we repudiate our past—far from it. Instead, we see those formulations as coming to us out of a cultural situation which we have now left. In our exodus culture we are called to a radically new understanding of the church's role.

On the one side there is the need for a new mode of formulation. As Robert Adolfs puts it, we must leave the essentialist dogmatic concepts that were used in the established culture of Christendom and we must learn to think and speak in existentialist historical terms.[15]

On the other side there is need to think of the church-world relation in much more humble and much more dynamic and secular fashion than we have been accustomed to in the past. It must be more humble in the sense that we must learn to stop thinking that the role of the church is to draw the world into the order of the church. We must cease thinking of the ultimate salvation of the world as the process by which Christ's Lordship over the body (Col. 1:18, Christ as head of the church) is expanded until at last it draws the whole world into its realm (Col. 2:10, Christ as head of the creation). Christ in his movement toward the fulfillment of his Lordship in the creation uses the community of those who already know him as Lord. The church is the servant of his struggle to bring this new and free life to expression in the communities of the world.[16] But the goal is the new life of the creation. The church is to be seen as an instrument that Christ uses for realizing the goal.

Our view of the church-world relation must also be more dynamic and secular than in the past. The struggle to reveal Christ's Lordship over creation must be related to the actual struggles of men in the social and political structures of our time. The church can be the church only as it is the community of obedience to Christ within the structures of life where human existence is actually played out.

The significance of this point can be gauged by J. A. T. Robinson's use of the slogan developed in the World Council of Churches' study on "The Missionary Structure of the Congregation": "God–World–Church." The slogan was developed in the study to point both to the humble position of the church—that it is the servant of God's mission in and for the world—and to the dynamic secular character of that servant role—that it must serve Christ in the midst of the struggles of men for a genuine worldly existence. The slogan was contrasted with the order of God–Church–World, symbolizing the attitude in which the church was seen as the place of God's primary relationship, with the world being saved by being drawn into the church. This old attitude, the slogan suggested, must be reversed—the church must be seen as the servant of God's relationship to the world.[17]

Robinson argues that this viewpoint is beginning to penetrate the work of both Protestant and Roman Catholic theologians but still has not penetrated the life of the churches. Nor has it penetrated the Decrees of Vatican II.

They still reflect the traditional theological order of God–Church–World (and indeed of God–Ministry–Church–World), as if God were primarily at work in his Church and through that on the world. Whereas, the biblical order (as the more radical material from the World Council of Churches' Commission on the Missionary Structure of the Congregation insists) is, rather, God–World–Church. The primary obedience of the Church is to find out where "the action" is, to be sensitive to the points at which God is working in history on the frontiers of social change, and there to serve him in it.[18]

So far, says Robinson, we have hardly begun to explore this perspective and to rethink the role of the church in its light. But we can discern the signs of a movement in this direction which cuts across traditional ecclesiastical barriers and which will allow for a genuinely lay theology, one that takes its start from the involvement of the people as the prophetic community within the secular structures, and that sees the role of the church as bringing to visibility the work of Christ as he struggles against the powers that dehumanize and seeks to open the way to the fully human community.[19]

At this point, as I have already suggested, we face a major difference over the way in which the church is called to exercise this humble, secular task. Balthasar emphasizes the direct role of the church as the pivotal sign for history, bringing the purpose of Christ to visibility in its struggle against the powers on the secular frontiers. Robinson (like Hoekendijk) emphasizes more the indirect role, with the church being available to join Christ where he is already struggling against the powers outside the visible boundaries of the church. Probably neither would exclude the point the other is making, but certainly the emphasis is different and the resultant attitude to the institution and mission of the church reflects that difference.

No attempt can be made at this stage to draw out farther the significance of this disagreement. It will reappear as the discussion unfolds. But perhaps a distinction made by Karl Rahner will help to set the stage. In contrasting the present diaspora servant role of the church with its dominant lordly role in the medieval period, Rahner says we should speak of the situation today both as one which "ought not to be" and as one which "must be."[20]

1. The church must be a minority "servant" group now because it has lost its power to command and is incapable of controlling the institutions of the world.

2. In one sense we can say this "ought not to be" since it is God's purpose that all men should accept Christ.

3. Again, it "ought not to be" that the church has lost much of its influence because it misused power when it had it.

4. In another sense we can say this "must be" because the world has come of age and no longer desires to have the church as mother ruling it from above. And in this development we can see the church called to help the world to hear Christ calling it to its mature role even when he is forced to the edge of history on to the cross, and, therefore, when his church too is forced to the edge of history.

5. Again, the church's diaspora situation is a "must" in the sense that the church must learn now to exist "out there" without strong institutional support in a cultural situation no longer shaped by the church, and in a lay situation where clergy have no privileged position. The church in our secular society must learn to reveal the mature "style of life" in which we reveal the meaning of

Christ's Lordship in the midst of secular affairs at the point where *only* the servant way is available, and *only* at the point where the faith is related to secular affairs.

In the chapters that follow we will be tracing the ways in which the thinking about the church and about its mission is currently being affected by this radical shift. Everywhere the evidence will be all too obvious that the writer himself is in the midst of this shift, and at some points the hold of the old will be far more apparent than at others. This book will also reveal the present dilemma of the church far more than it will reveal the resolution of the dilemma. The hope can only be that the direction in which Christ is leading his church has been properly sensed, and that the reader can be helped to become a participant in the struggle of the church to be available to its Lord as he uses it to reveal his Lordship to the world.

CHAPTER II

The Church as Event: The Servant of God's Happening-in-the-World

It is a favorite emphasis today to speak of the church as "event." The church is a movement—a pilgrim people moving across time and space in participation in the mission of Jesus Christ. It is an event because this participation has to happen, and that happening is not something that is guaranteed in the institutional heritage.

Beneath the agreement on the church as event, however, there is disagreement on the relation of the happening to the given continuities of the life of the covenant people. This problem of the relationship between "event" and "institution" is suggestively explored by F. J. Leenhardt through the Biblical tension between the Abraham motif (event) and the Moses motif (institution).[1] Abraham and his departure from all securities, going out as a pilgrim in obedience to the call of God, is a pivotal symbol throughout the Biblical story for the event character of the people of God. As the people of God they are constantly being called to stretch out beyond the institutionally given to the final purpose and plan of God. They are the people of God only as they continue to move out in search of "the city which has foundations, whose builder and maker is God" (Heb. 11:10).

But there is a contrasting motif. Moses received from God the law, and with the law a rich institutional life was given. The people of God may live only in the constantly renewed movement out of the securities of their past into the promises of God's future. But for that pilgrimage God gives to their lives a characteristic style and form so that they will have the training and provisions they need for the journey (Word and Sacraments, law and cult), and so that the style and form of life can act as a sign to the nations of the destiny God has in mind for all the nations.

The two motifs—event and institution—are inseparable from each other. And yet the two are also in severe tension with each other and on occasion (e.g., the time of the exile) they can reach the breaking point. It is the attitude toward the tension that is vital. Paul, in Galatians, insists on the priority of the Abrahamic covenant. Institution is at the service of event, and where the form of the institution is standing in the way of the happening of contemporary obedience to God's call to his people to move on with him in history, then the priority of event must be recognized. (Gal. 3:5–29.)

In our time this question has taken on new urgency. We are in something like a new exile situation. Our churches have been taken out of the securities of the Christendom situation. We have been forced to leave many of the institutional forms that were characteristic of the period of the Christian West. As the pilgrim people moving through the previous thousand years, our fathers used the social institutions, the thought forms, the cultural patterns of their day as the vehicles for their missionary witness, and the rich and complex life of that "Christian civilization" were the result. Now that we are leaving behind these forms— as pilgrim people we use them without obligation, and fold up our tents and move on when God shifts the scene of action—we have the problem of deciding what is the continuing institutional life that we need. The event character of our life has priority; the Abraham covenant precedes the covenant with Moses. And so we can speak of the church, to quote from the report of the study on "The Missionary Structure of the Congregation," as a "happening 'on the road' from one event to the next." The church has to be free in this way because it is in the service of the One who is the hidden center of history's moving action. Nevertheless, the church must have institutional forms; it is called to bring the hidden meaning of life to visibility, and its Lord equips it with continuing forms which express both his care for it and his purpose for it.

What then are those "given continuities" that are provided for the church for its pilgrimage? The problem is that they have no fixed form. The church realized after the death and resurrection of Jesus that it could no longer center its life on a fixed temple of stones (or a fixed body of law, or a fixed body of doctrine, or a fixed cultus), because it is the living temple of Christ's moving presence. And so the task is to explore the event character of the church and from this priority point to ask what form the continuing traveling provisions (such as Word and cult) should now assume. The question is how the institutional life can best order the people of God for their availability in the event of contemporary obedience.

THE PRESENT SITUATION ON THE CHURCH-WORLD FRONTIER

At the time of the Reformation the church problem became acute. The Reformers' problem was not so much that the institutions in which the church was living were archaic but, rather, that the church was not using those institutions for Christ's purpose. Their problem then was, How can the church become the true church again? And their answer was, When it truly preaches the Word and administers the Sacraments.

For us too the church problem has become acute. But for us the question is far more radical. If we continue to live in the received institutions, we are in danger of being stranded on the shores of the stream of change. So our question is, How can a church that still lives in many of the institutional forms it created in the lost religious age —the age of Christendom—reshape its life so that it is freed for a real encounter with the present secular age?

It is not the place here to rehearse the characteristics of this radical change in man's relationship to the world. Many aspects of it will appear as we proceed, but the general story now is familiar.[2] It is sufficient here to remind ourselves of something of its significance for the church. It means, in short, that the answer to the church problem at the time of the Reformation can no longer be the answer to our church problem. They asked, How can we be sure that the church truly exists within the institutions of the church? The answer they gave was, We can be sure that where the Word is truly preached and where the Sacraments are administered rightly, Christ will create faith and gather his faithful. In their Christendom situation that answer had explosive power. But in our exodus situation the question becomes one of *where* the church is the church. It is the problem of how we can move out with Christ into the secular world, and what the shapes of our obedience must be as we seek to be his servant presence in the midst of the shapes of need and hope that charterize our age.

It is for this reason that the event character of the church has now come to the fore, and it is for this reason that stress has been placed upon the way that event is leading us today to a major institutional reshaping of the life of the church. The answers being suggested are not meant to be final answers to the ecclesiological question. In fact, the stress is that there are no final answers. Ecclesiology's task is simply to point to where the answers are to be found, for the answer is in the event and cannot be fully predicted.

Where, then, are we to look for the church? The church is, the event theology suggests, where the people of God are taking servant shape around the needs and hopes of the world—as servants of Christ and therefore as servants of men. Behind this suggestion can be seen the major assumption: that the church is called to move into the world as Christ still moves in the world. Christ did not come as one dispensing preestablished answers, the bringer of a changeless eternal order into our changing temporal order. He came as a full participant in history. He came as a silent child; he grew up at the bosom of the world. He came as the one whose freedom was his complete freedom for the needs of the world, moving out from behind the barricades of assumed safety and order to reach the excluded with the community-creating power of servant love. The foolishness of that risky servant love he revealed as the secret clue that opened the way to the true future—a future in which all mankind would finally share in the "new creation" of the one family of God's love. Beyond its apparent defeat, he revealed the power of this love to create in his disciples the faith and courage to become participants in the servant way. And that participation is the church—"the followers of the way."

What we have in this kind of ecclesiology then is a pointing: it seeks to direct us to the place where we will find the way of the church. But to do that effectively it has to fill out these directions considerably, not only by telling us more about this servant shape of Christ in which we are called to participate, but also by telling us more about the shapes of need and hope in our world where this servant form appears. In fact, the suggestion is, it is with those shapes of need and hope in our world which we must begin, for Christ began by growing up into his world and making himself available in the midst of the particular needs and hopes of his time.[3]

For this reason "The Missionary Structure of the Congregation" study adopted another slogan in its attempt to direct us to the place where the church event can be expected to occur. "Let the world write the agenda." We must be the listening church before we can be the speaking church. We must discern the shapes of need and hope before we can take the shape of servant love and before we can point with any accuracy to the hidden work of Christ as he continues to work in history now, as he worked openly in history in the days of his flesh.

This catchy slogan, however, has its problems. If we are to let the world write the agenda, we must return to the New Testament to get some clues as to how this happens. How did Jesus of Nazareth read the agenda the world was writing?

When we return to the New Testament the problems rapidly become obvious. "The world" there is normally viewed with suspicion as a reality whose agenda is designed to lead us astray. The general judgment is that if you open yourself to the world around you, you will become a slave to its inner dynamics, be led away from God's purpose for his creation, and be radically corrupted or dehumanized. It is not just that there are suspicious characters at large in the world, dragging down the level of its life. It is not just that the world is run by groups whose institutional self-concern makes them blind to crying needs that their establishment systems are failing to meet. The judgment goes even farther. The total "form of this world" is judged as a power that enslaves us all, unless we are freed from its inner dynamic. To quote three typical witnesses:

Paul: "The god of this world has blinded the minds of the unbelievers." (II Cor. 4:4.)

James: "Do you not know that friendship with the world is enmity with God?" (James 4:4.)

John: "Everything the world affords, all that panders to the appetites, or entices the eyes, all the glamour of its life, springs not from the Father but from the godless world." (I John 2:16, NEB.)

Nor can it be said that these sayings from the letters of the New Testament reflect an otherworldliness of the religious thought of that time which had not yet been fully converted by the world-affirming love that Jesus represents and that John caught up in his famous confession about Jesus: "God so loved the world that he gave his only Son" (John 3:16). For it seems clear that Jesus taught his disciples that the way of life represented in society—perhaps our term "the establishment" says it best—is a way of life organized away from God's purpose for mankind. If we allow ourselves to be carried along on the stream of life as it is, then it follows that we will inevitably be carried astray from God's way. Only he who is prepared to lose his life can save it. We have to die to the typical worldly life if we hope to rise into his free life.

This "art of dying," as the old theologies used to call it, is the secret center to discipleship. Dying to the world is the birth-point of the church—the community that is for

c

the world as it should be and that points to the way in which the world can be freed from its inauthentic form. This death and new birth are a gift of grace, a conversion. That is the very reason why the church is an event—a happening—and not an establishment. It is a free life that has to be constantly created as men are freed from the drifting, self-centered form of "natural" worldly life, and freed for life with Christ as he opens the way to the new future.

This "event" view of life, however, has its secular echo in a good deal of contemporary thinking. If we are to be free for the possibilities of our scientific-technological society, we must move away from establishment categories to event. For example, Walter J. Ong, S.J., in his suggestive book *In the Human Grain,* writes: "We know today that the cosmos is not a perfectly wound clock, not a neat design with everything in its place. . . . The cosmos can be seen today as an event, a happening. It is something 'going on.' "[4] This attitude is connected with the vast change in man's attitude toward the world, which is spoken of under the rubric of "coming-of-age"; and Father Ong, in common with many contemporary writers, connects this changed attitude to the influence of the Hebrew-Christian view of God's relation to the world: God is the one Creator whose order for the world is one that is open to the working out of his purpose. To enable man to participate in the working out of this purpose, God gives him a participation in his transcendence. The event character of science and philosophy—the death of closed systems and the emphasis on historical categories in which the future can be grasped with its creative possibilities—can be seen then as a "reflection" into human affairs of the understanding of life provided by the Biblical story.

But the question is, while we see this coming-of-age as a sign of the working out of God's purpose, must we not say that the event reality of life on this scientific level depends for its health on the event in human existence by which we are freed from the naturally selfish world? Is it not true that without this, the great release in creativity on the scientific level simply raises the demonic dangers? In other words, the church is called to be the sign to the world of its true destiny, the event that illuminates the truth of all events.

This means, then, that when we "let the world write the agenda," we are not to let it write in its own answers. Our ecclesiology leads us to take seriously the contemporary questions, but as we move out with Christ we are to be ready to see even the questions in a new light. We must learn to see the world, as Tertullian put it, "with grace-healed eyes," or as Bonhoeffer put it, "with Christ between."

With all those provisos, however, we still begin with the world in its own agenda. So today, for example, we must explore the meaning of the rise of our scientific secular society; the meaning of the death of the old religions and metaphysical frameworks of understanding; the meaning of the pressures toward a universal society, with the cracking of the old caste systems and enclosed racial communities; the meaning of the revolution of hope, by which the masses are seeing for the first time the possibility that they can participate in a fully human life in this world; the meaning of the resistances to new hopes as the possessors of privilege react with fear to the processes of radical change that threaten the structures of their privilege. These and the many other urgent world agenda questions confront us with our ecclesiological question: How

can we become the servant presence in the midst of these
hopes and fears, serving to point the way to the future
into which Christ is leading the world? How can the
church be an event that points to those events through
which the world can appropriate the promises that God
offers it in the purpose for the creation that Christ reveals?

Something of the meaning of the changed theological
position in what is being called the postmodern secular
world, is illustrated in the thesis of Balthasar's book *Christ
the Heart of the World*.[5] Previous generations, he tells us,
all lived in a religious world. Theirs was a "theological
cosmos" and their lives were played out in a total theological drama in which earth, heaven, hell, and purgatory were
the major locations. But in our awareness of the world,
the theological cosmos has given way to a "physical cosmos." The drama of our existence is played out on the
earth itself. If the old theological drama is to mean anything to postmodern man, it must be transferred from the
old familiar theological cosmic stage and must be brought
to life on the stage of history.

For the church the transfer means a painful transition.
We are tempted to protest and to insist that the old stage
is still the real one and that modern man has so restricted
the scenes that the representation of the full drama is
impossible until his secularizing direction is reversed. But
not so, says Balthasar. The Biblical story itself helps us to
see the collapse of that familiar theological cosmic stage
as the work of God, and as potential liberation. Now that
man is freed for full attention to God's purpose for history,
the church can be freed from its remaining fixation with
religious places and concerns, and freed to concentrate on
Christ's living purpose within the processes of history.

This thesis we are familiar with in Protestant circles in

the post-Bonhoeffer stream.[6] But it is important to see that this is not a peculiarly Protestant angle of vision. It is, in fact, in large measure because these developments have dissolved the significance of the different church answers Protestants and Catholics gave to the questions of the sixteenth century that the ecumenical movement of the twentieth century is bringing us together. The one world we share (the *oikoumenē*) is enabling us to be brought together across our past differences with the possibility that here we can receive a common church response to the questions of the world. Now there is a chance that we can more effectively represent God's one purpose to his one world.

In another of his books, *The Razing of the Ramparts*, Balthasar traces the changing forms of church obedience that are required by this movement of God in breaking down the old theological cosmos.[7] The church is now called, he says, to the breaking down of the encapsulated attitudes in which she thought of herself as providing sacred spaces for the divine invasion into the secular. We have to shift now to an open attitude in which the church is in the midst of the key events of our time as the servant of God's presence in those events. To give personal expression to this, in 1950 Balthasar left the Society of Jesus to devote himself to secular institutes so that (as he wrote) "the counsels of perfection may begin to break through in Christ-formation in the forms of the world."

This direction of ecclesiology to which we have been pointing is a movement away from yesterday's question of where the true church is to be found within the established order of Christendom, to today's question of where the living church must occur as witness to Christ's presence in the secular world. The movement (still in a transition

stage) is illustrated in the treatment of ecclesiology at
Vatican Council II. In its initial form as it came from the
preparatory theological commission, the schema *De Ecclesia* was traditional. The symbol at the heart of the document was "the body of Christ," and the interpretation of
that symbol was hierarchical, stressing the metaphysical
character of the church's life as a given institutional continuity through which the eternal order is sacramentally
infused into the disorder of our temporal world. But under
the momentum of the Council, the traditional metaphysical starting point was replaced by a historical starting
point. The primary symbol became that of "the people
of God" moving on its pilgrim way.[8]

What is at stake in this transition? Perhaps two illus-
trations will indicate something of its significance.

1. Cultural analysts such as Walter Ong are speaking of
the underlying change as a move from a society of *order* to
a society of *movement* or constant change. It is a move
from the relatively static culture of classical and medieval
life where man's self-awareness was expressed in spatial,
visual symbols (space being the great symbol of order) to
the open, dynamic culture of contemporary life where
man's self-awareness is increasingly temporal. Man no
longer sees life within a fixed framework; he is aware of
life as a "project" which is being realized in an emerging
future.

Now if (as Ong and many other theologians are saying)
this change to the open, future-regarding view is insepar-
ably related to the Hebrew-Christian understanding of
history, it follows that the dissolution of the old ecclesiologies, in favor of event or happening views is a development to be expected and welcomed. It reflects the growing
victory of the historical view of existence that character-

izes the Biblical understanding of God's relation to the world. But more important still, the event ecclesiology will serve to free the Christian community from overconcern with its own order and life to more active participation in the struggles of the world as the servant of Christ's historical purpose.

2. From another angle, the change has been described in terms of the collapse of a sacral framework which men previously felt essential to life's meaning. Men assumed that there was a sacral order surrounding the temporal order from which authoritative truths and sacred influences were introduced into life through divinely-given religious channels. But now this old sacral framework has collapsed, delivering life into historical categories, and delivering man into a freer way of thinking and acting. Under the sacral order attitude, society is looked upon in basically conservative terms. It is assumed that society must have structures that reflect the eternal order and that it is held from falling into chaos only when that authoritative order is respected. The church tends to be conceived as the guardian of the sacral order. The collapse of the sacral world involves a movement from this basically conservative view of life to a future-oriented, change-expecting view of existence. When ecclesiology is changed accordingly, then the church is freed from its conservative role and freed for its task amid the radical changes of our times.

In case we are tempted to think of this significance only in abstract terms, we will try to illustrate its importance from *The Autobiography of Malcolm X*. Robert Bone's review of the book in *The New York Times Book Review* of September 11, 1966, was headlined, "A Black Man's Quarrel with the Christian God." In it he explored the Black Muslim's life as a "metaphysical revolt" against the

white man's God—or better, against the God of a church
that gave ontological sanction to the white-dominated
social order of Christendom. Malcolm X's attitude he
summarizes as follows:

The Christian religion is the tribal religion of white Europe.
Since the time of the Crusades, the Christian church has in-
stigated, championed, and proclaimed as holy the white man's
depredations into Africa. Throughout the centuries, and in
every corner of the globe, the church has been the willing
instrument of white power. She has been guilty of sanctifying
white supremacy, blessing the white man's wars of conquest,
and justifying in the name of God slavery and segregation.
Without pity or remorse the Christian church has aided and
abetted the white man in his criminal designs upon the
colored world.

Of course, it is easy to show that this representation is a
caricature of the Christian faith as it is mirrored in the
Bible. Even as a representation of the story of the church in
the post-Crusade period of imperialist Western expansion,
this is a cruel, one-sided distortion. But there is an important point in this distorted picture. The Christian
church of the West—particularly after the Crusades—did
become closely identified with a hierarchical structure of
society in which religious and metaphysical justification
was given to the established structures of white Western
culture. Now, as a result, the church finds itself struggling
with great difficulty and pain to break free from sub-
Christian social prejudices deeply ingrained in their ad-
herents through these centuries of metaphysical and social
conditioning.

The change in ecclesiology seeks to point to that needed
repentance. The case being made is that the casting off of
the traditional metaphysical sacral views of the church
institution is an essential aspect of the repentance by

which we turn away from the inherited caste structures of society that our hierarchical views have sanctified. That change has been taking place gradually since the Reformation, but the new ecclesiology seeks to carry it through so that the blasphemy of churches serving as bulwarks for the dying social order may be overcome, and so that the church may be free to be on the frontier where God is opening the way to the hope of the future.

A little more of the church's story in the white West may help to strengthen our awareness of the crucial importance of what is involved here. This hierarchical, metaphysical, conservative view of life was reinforced by the two-realms view of God's relation to history. God brought the demands of his order into our temporal order through the two arms of his one government: church and state. The church was responsible for the sacred dimension, the state for the secular order; and in this dual arrangement of the establishment the church was little inclined to bring any challenge to the structures of secular life. In fact, it reinforced them with its divine authority.

With the Reformation there were revisions in this two-realms view. The Lutheran, Reformed, and Anglican Churches each had their particular variants as the traditional structural attitudes were revised under the pressures of middle-class society. But we must not forget how essentially conservative the revisions still were. Cast your mind back, for example, to the Anglican situation in 1603 with James I coming down from Scotland to mount the British throne and imperiously rejecting Presbyterian and Puritan views of the role of the king and of the relation of the church to the inherited feudal structures. James simply reaffirmed the long medieval tradition of the divine right of kings. God has given society this sacral order, and the hierarchical structure is anchored above in metaphysical timelessness. Only this eternal order impinging on time prevents the social order from being dragged down into the chaos of time's swirling stream. All depends upon the eternal givenness of God's providential ordering of society and the sacralizing of that order through the sacramental structures of the church. Bishop and king are the twin pillars of God's order—a revolt against either the religious or the social structure is a revolt against God.

Certainly this feudal view was modified in the Lutheran and Reformed traditions as the relatively static feudal period gave way to the more dynamic period of imperialism. But the view that the church was the place of entrance for God's eternal order into the world of dangerous temporal disorder, and the view that the church and state were two arms of God's one government whose task was essentially a stabilizing and conservative one—these attitudes continued in large degree. Under this view the church can do much to civilize and purify the given social order. However, that is precisely its limited role. It purifies men, and through their purified lives it humanizes the given social structures. But the church keeps to its religious role and leaves the task of secular order to the state, thus aiding the resistance to any pressure for radical social change.

This traditional ecclesiology was increasingly challenged by more radical Christian thinkers of the ecclesiastical left, but in general it has held its place in the mainstream churches until our day. Even where the hierarchical metaphysical framework that had supported it collapsed, as in the middle-class Protestant world of the West, the predominant Pietism that took over reinforced much of the conservative social role of the church. In Pietism grace was seen as a power that invades the heart and gives new energies to man, but obedience was not seen as joining Christ in a work of fundamental restructuring of the social, cultural, and national forms of human existence.

Now that conservative view of the role of the church is under serious challenge. With the breakdown of Christendom, with the revolt of Asia and Africa against the Christian West, and with the challenge of the dispossessed colored to the inherited dominance of the white Christian world, it has become increasingly apparent that the hierarchical views of church and society and the pietist limitations of the church's role to the religious order are hindrances to an understanding of the positive role of the church in the processes of change.

It is, of course, not only forces from outside the Christian West that have challenged the old conservative views of the church. Within the Western culture itself a major pressure toward openness to the future has built up through the emergence of science technology. Walter Ong is of the opinion that an even stronger pressure has come with the change from the print-centered culture to the oral-aural culture.[9] Print orients us to an ordered, fixed view of life. Our electronic-media age takes us into the dynamic temporal world of living language. Ong illustrates his point from the response to the publication of *Webster's Third New International Dictionary* in which the change in language from "correct" fixed forms to the changing forms of living language was accepted as the norm. There was a strong popular revulsion which reflected the deep-lying recognition that here the transition from a fixed-order view of life to a dynamic open view of existence was being accepted and affirmed. Right-wing resistances to all such changes must be understood in this light. "The alphabetically-conditioned psyche," he writes, "is terrorized by the fact that Webster III has abandoned the solid world of space for the uncertainties of time."[10]

Before we proceed to the more formal reassessment of the transition to the new ecclesiology brought about by all these changes, a few programmatic comments on some of its probable effects may be in place.

1. It seems clear that it is leading to *a fierce struggle* between those who see the new ecclesiology as the result of Christ's work in history calling us into new forms of obedience and those who see its departure from the ordered view of the past as a dangerous radicalism that will drain the church of its religious substance and draw the church out of its given spiritual realm into the struggles of the secular world, with the consequent loss of the basic truth the church must offer: that only changed hearts are a remedy for the disorders caused by sin.

2. The new ecclesiology will involve us in crucial struggles not only over the *places* of our obedience—in such issues as race, poverty, peace—but over the *forms* through which the obedience is to be expressed. Pressure is mounting in the churches for movement away from the relatively static institutional patterns of church life which we have inherited from the rural societies of the past to the more mobile pluralistic forms of mission that are now needed for Christian presence in the variety of worlds in our urban-technological society.[11] Most members still think of the church as fixed in its presence in a changeless local church, and as fixed in the mode of its presence through the traditional expressions of Word, Sacrament, and godly fellowship. But now there is increasing awareness that more mobile and varied forms of presence are needed and that the modes of that presence must also display a new

variety if the church is to be free to serve as the identifying presence of "the man for others" at the points of emerging hope and continuing need.

In a typical piece of writing, Harvey Cox asks what must be the forms of missionary presence in our emerging urban society. He answers:

It is our brief experience in the black ghettos of America which will now provide the most valuable experience. In the ghettos we have learned a style of mission which provides the only viable model for mission in the vast Afro-Asian ghetto. What have we learned? We have learned that God wants His people to identify themselves unequivocally with the cry of the poor for justice now. He allows His word to be heard in the ghetto only when those who speak it share the existence of those who hear it. He has taught us that we must be willing to disappear, to see our buildings, our property and our institutional safeguards threatened and even destroyed so that an authentic link with the people can be fashioned. God has taught us that, like John the Baptist, we must decrease if He is to increase. He has taught us that in the institutional temple of religion, perhaps no stone can be left standing on another before the new temple of the body of Christ emerges. As long as we try to keep one or two stones pasted together as a possible escape route, we only succeed in postponing that indispensable identification with those whom God has sent us to serve.[12]

Too radical in its attitude toward church institutions? Maybe, but the theological point is the vital thing: that the church is called to be present with Christ as he moves within the struggles of history to work out his purpose for the world, whereas too often we have suggested that the church brings Christ to man at sacred times and places that stand apart from the radical struggles of history.

3. This new ecclesiology, we have said, will direct us to new *places* of obedience and new *forms* of obedience; leading to identification with particular people and groups

struggling for historical air. It will also lead us into the struggle for *new community* life in which the church seeks to be the sign of the society of God that transcends old tribalisms and breaks through the limitations of our national communities. This call to press on to a community life that not only transcends old color, caste, and class barriers but also breaks through the fiercely held autonomies of national life will require far more imaginative ecumenical strategies than those which are so far represented by our church union initiatives. These are mainly limited to pulling together present ecclesiastical forms by merger, therefore, accepting much of the present color, caste, and class barriers and making almost no attempt to reach out through the ultimately more destructive national barriers which stand in the way of the movement to the open universal community to which alone the peace of God is given.

It is at this point that we will face the real test—the test of the ability of the church to be the event in which the world can see a happening that will give substance to the hope for a community that overcomes racism, tribalism, nationalism. Here we wrestle not against flesh and blood but against principalities and powers which will be defeated only through costly struggles—only by the way of the cross.

This leads to a final comment on the practical meaning of this new ecclesiology. We must not think that this insistence on the church's being sought at the places of commitment to Christ in the midst of his movement through history represents the acceptance of an optimistic view of historical progress. Some of the terms being used to describe the changes in man's relation to the world may mislead us in that direction. When it is said that man has come of age and can now live without the authority of outside metaphysical structures and external religious assurance; and when it is said that man is delivered into full responsibility for history, it may appear that man has at last come through the worst vicissitudes of history and is now entering the final stretch with the goal in sight.

We need to be careful here. In Paul's discussion in Gal., ch. 4, we can see the way to put these statements about man-come-of-age into their right perspective. There he argues that before Christ came men had assumed that human life was under the control of the elemental spirits of the universe. Now we see that Christ has made us free of these, and that history has only one Lord—Christ himself. We are, therefore, not children anymore, under the tutelage of those outside authorities. We now have to become mature and accept responsibility for our lives in history, with Christ as the guide of our pilgrimage.

Here we are given the interpretative clue to the meaning of the death of the old metaphysics and of past conservative religious attitudes. We are free for history and free to move out with Christ as he opens up the future to his purpose. But that does not lead us into any naïve optimism. To move out with Christ means to move out into a deep struggle. We can know that the elemental spirits (or their modern equivalents of racism, tribalism, nationalism, etc.) are overcome by Christ and that we can be freed to leave them behind. But if Christ's future is to be opened up, he still has to break his way past the incredible resistance of those who find their false securities in hanging on to these childish attitudes. As we join him in that struggle we must know what the cost is likely to be.

In the Biblical picture of historical development, we are given at the beginning a commandment to man: he is told to take responsibility for the earth and to subdue it by bringing forth its full potentialities. But man's response to God's creation commandment is ambivalent and touched with tragedy. Man is called to build a city. The first city builder is Cain, however, and the first city achievement is the Tower of Babel. Nevertheless, the vision is kept alive until Jesus of Nazareth at last stimulates the vision of the ultimate city, given in the book of Revelation. But Jesus made it clear that the goal is reachable only through costly struggles leading through the death of false ambitions and limiting systems and along the servant path that leads to the open community in which all nations, tongues, races, and classes will find their unity.

The promise of history must be seen then as a bittersweet promise. It is not open to direct appropriation, but can be received only as a gift through the gate of historical repentance. The church must be seen in this picture, for the church is called to be the pilgrim community of representative penitents, repenting of the excluding forms our human sin has taken. As a pilgrim group the church lives by the constant renewal of that penitence. Only in that way can it be freed from the false ambitions and the limited forms of community into which its members are constantly drawn through their life in "the world." Only through that penitent way are they free to be the servant presence of Christ, who leads his pilgrim people on as the sign of the fulfillment of his purpose for all.

The church is an event, a happening that Christ brings about from day to day. We have no promise that Israel will be faithful, that we can look at the given institution called church and say that it represents the purpose of Christ for history. We have only the promise that Christ will be faithful and that as he works in history there will always be a remnant who have not bowed the knee to Baal nor surrendered to the limited ways of the world. We have no promise that even these faithful will resist the temptations. We have only the promise that his call will come again and again to die to the false forms of the world and to rise with him to the journey to his free future.

The church is the church as it is renewed day by day, dying to the limited forms of the world's past and rising to the freedom of serving Christ as he opens up the world's future.

D

CHAPTER III

The Traditional Views Reexamined:
Catholic, Classical Protestant,
and Free Church Views

"Comparative ecclesiology" was the order of the day in the first stage of the modern ecumenical movement. The churches probed their own self-understanding and sought to explain themselves to one another in the hope that as they compared their views they would be able to discover the tradition behind the traditions, the God-given original unity behind the historical disunities. In the Faith and Order movement this process was carefully developed through the work of its international commissions.[1]

Beyond that official study approach, there have also been the proposals for particular church unions in which attempts have been made to find ways by which the varying ecclesiologies of the negotiating churches could be brought together and their differences transcended in the development of an ecclesiology all could accept.[2] In the formation of the Church of South India (CSI) in 1947, the Basis of Union was an attempt to affirm the essential elements of the Catholic tradition of the Anglican communion, the Reformed tradition of Presbyterian churches, and the left-wing Protestant tradition of Congregational churches,[3] and to find the way by which churches that came out of these varied histories could grow together into a living form of unity suited to the present setting in which the Christian witness is to be continued. A similar approach is represented in the Blake proposal from which the Consultation on Church Union (COCU) took its beginnings.[4] The basic proposal made by Eugene Carson Blake was that there are three major ecclesiologies that have to be drawn together if an effective form of union is to be fashioned in which the churches can be united for their one mission. The uniting church must be "truly catholic, truly reformed, and truly evangelical."

We can see, then, both in the broad study method and in the actual attempts to forge forms of unity, a dual approach. There is an essential movement back into our divided past in order to be faithful to the words of God that are represented in our history, and there is also an essential movement forward as we seek to hear the word of God to us in our situation as he calls us into the unity of witness which is his will for us now. To attempt to move forward without reaching back would be to risk a church in which the rich givenness of Christian faith and life was seriously eroded. Constantly we must hear the word "remember," by which we are forced to recognize in the given shape of God's action in the past the essential clues to a recognition of his action in the present. But to limit ourselves to the movement back within our past traditions is to risk a church that will be a magnificent monument to past glories but will not be open to the needs of the present.

Christ comes to us not only out of the past, out of the story of his redeeming work already accomplished, but also out of the future, summoning us to new forms of obedience as he continues to work out the redemption he has revealed. For that reason the movement back should not be undertaken in separation from the movement forward. The answers from the past become luminous when drawn out by our present questions, while our present questions themselves are reshaped by the word the past speaks to us. This is hardly surprising. It means that our eyes are opened to the present Christ and his demands when we ask our questions of present obedience in the context of his appearance in the first century. It means also that our eyes are opened to deeper meanings of his past presence as we seek the new forms of our discipleship in the very different conditions of today. Christ has many things to tell us now which could not be spoken in the days of his flesh but had to wait until the questions of today could be addressed to him. The Spirit gives us these further truths as truths already hidden within Christ's past revelation. (John 16:12-15.)

In this slow struggle in the modern ecumenical movement to find the right relation between these two inseparable processes, several major developments have emerged which should serve to illumine our path in search of an ecclesiology for our day.

THE ECCLESIASTICAL "FAMILIES"

An attempt was inevitable to bring some order into our investigation of the many ecclesiological strands by classifying them into major "families." A rough consensus has emerged that we can usefully divide them into three major streams of tradition:

1. The *Catholic* view, sometimes called the "horizontal" view, seems to place its prior emphasis upon the "given continuity" of the life of the church within history.

Its initial stress is upon the claim that Christ has given the church guaranteed historical characteristics by which he keeps the church continuously present in the world and through which he keeps his redemptive presence continuously available to man. There are vital differences of emphasis between the various representatives of this horizontal view—Roman Catholic, Orthodox, Anglo-Catholic —but there is the common assertion that the true church must be found in the context of the visibly continuous ministry, creeds, liturgy, and Sacraments.

2. The *classical Protestant* view is sometimes called the "objective vertical" view, because it places priority of emphasis upon the way the church is continuously called into being "from above" through the preaching of the Word and sustained in being from above by the given life of the Sacraments. Again there are vital differences of emphasis among the various representatives of this view— Lutheran and Reformed—but there is the common emphasis that we must look first, not to historical continuities visible to the eye of man, but to the event of faith in which Christ continuously calls his church into existence through the true preaching of the Word and the due administration of the Sacraments.

3. The *free church Protestant* view is sometimes called the "subjective vertical" view, because it places priority of emphasis upon the free response of believers in the Spirit and upon the need for us to be open to the possibility that Christ will call out new forms of faith and obedience in apparent disregard of the niceties of visible continuity. There is a considerable range of differences between the wide assortment of free churches, and yet there seems to be an obvious family similarity that characterizes them in their differences.

Now it is easy (and undoubtedly justified) to insist that a healthy ecclesiology today will need to include all three emphases. It is illuminating, too, to suggest that these three emphases can be brought together in a Trinitarian reconciliation:[5]

— the Catholic horizontal view, representing the symbol of "God the Father" as the providential continuity of God's unbroken care for his creation;

— the classical Protestant objective vertical view, representing the symbol of "God the Son" as the One who constantly recalls the world to its true center and who summons it out of its false worldly continuities into the redeemed continuities of his original purpose;

— the free church Protestant subjective vertical view, representing the symbol of "God the Spirit" bringing unpredictable responses out of the sluggish stream of history, but in such a way that yesterday's stream of renewal becomes tomorrow's pool of inertia out of which yet new forms of obedience have to be drawn.

THE TRINITARIAN STRUCTURE OF THE CHURCH

This family view would seem to suggest that there is a Trinitarian reality of the church that has tended to fragment from time to time, but requires that the rediscovery of unity be sought within the wholeness of the Trinitarian work of God. To some it has appeared that promising results could accrue if we were to explore the traditional Trinitarian formulations for the light they can throw on the proper relation between the three motifs which have become so sadly separated over the course of the centuries.

For example, take the doctrine of "perichoresis"—the teaching that the three persons of the Trinity "interpenetrate" in the unity of the one life of God. This suggests the way in which the three ecclesiological emphases must interpenetrate in an adequate doctrine of the church. But what does this have to say about the right relation between these three emphases? Here we may call in the doctrine of the "procession" of the life of the Trinity, or perhaps (if we accept the Western clause) also the "filioque." If the Son "proceeds" from the Father, and the Spirit from the Father and the Son, this may suggest that the objective vertical view has to be held within the prior framework of the Father's concern for the whole created order, with its created continuities and cosmic context, and that the subjective vertical must be protected from uncontrolled freedom by being placed under proper Christological control.[6]

Hesitations enter concerning this speculative line. What is the status of these Trinitarian formulations and how great is the interpretative value? That they represent a highly creative "projection" of the meaning of the Christ event into the Greek language and classical thought forms we may allow. But before we can use these insights with any measure of control today, we have to translate them from those older metaphysical categories into the historical categories of our time.

"START WITH CHRIST"

At this point a more historical starting point suggests itself. The historical center of the doctrine of the Trinity lies in its concern with Jesus of Nazareth. It was the conviction that the reality of God, with its radical promises and demands, had here broken through in history that impelled the church along the path of Trinitarian speculation. Similarly, the life of the church emerged out of that historical center as a response to the Christ event.

It is this conviction which lies behind the suggestion

that emerged at the Faith and Order meeting at Lund in 1952 that the right place for the churches to begin their common search for the one church is with Christology. "The nearer we come to Christ," the suggestion ran, "the nearer we come to each other." Or, to put it another way, the church's true unity can be given it only when it looks beyond its own divided life to Christ, its head.

There can be little doubt that this approach has resulted in some important gains within Faith and Order.[7] One effect was the reminder that the path to true unity cannot be found by putting together the pieces of past tradition into an ecclesiastical jigsaw puzzle. The church of the present can be found not in its own past alone but in its Living Lord. While the traditions must be examined for the clues they can give us in the search for present obedience to Christ, we must not forget that the unity needed now is an event which occurs at the point of true response to Christ today. That this response will have common features with the responses of the past we can reasonably expect. The Christ event has a recognizable shape. We must search for the common features that mark the moments of past obedience, while being open to the mystery of how they will be taken up into a new form as the people of God seek to follow Christ into the servant tasks of the present.

EXPLORING THE BIBLICAL PICTURE

In this search for the common features of past church events and for characteristics of the ways in which these continuities are taken up in new forms in changing situations, what is the status of the New Testament picture of the church? In those pages we can see how the church in the first century took on a variety of forms. The response to Christ within varied situations led to the emergence of different forms of ministry, liturgy, preaching, doctrinal formulation. What does this have to say to the church of today about its search for unity?

By giving the Bible canonical status, the church has (in one sense) lifted this picture of the church above the continuing stream of tradition. It has given to the primal, formative moments of the tradition normative status in relation to the rest of the tradition. But we must not take that to mean that it constitutes a "timeless" norm, so that we should seek to reproduce that picture of the church in every time and place. Instead, it is normative in the sense that this first response to Christ within the stream of history can provide the clues to future responses to Christ within that stream.

This helps us to see what the interpretative task is. We are to explore that first moving picture with all its variety. We must not seek to harmonize that variety into a single picture that would then provide the basis for unity. The variety is the message. We must seek for clues to our response to Christ within the varied situation of our time within their response to the varied situation of that time. This requires us to shuttle back and forth between the two settings, putting our questions to it and its questions to us, and (with the help of the continuing story of the church to check our intuitions) to seek to discern from this encounter the forms and shapes of the church's obedience today.

From the New Testament variety we ask: How much continuity is needed in the life of the church from one situation to another? What common features mark the life of the church in those different first-century settings? Is the relation between continuity and freedom describable?

It is to this Biblical exploration that we now turn. But a warning is needed. It is one thing to point, as we have, to the way in which the New Testament pictures a living church in the process of obedience. But as we explore that picture, the temptation still is to turn a movement, described in the process of faithful response to particular situations, into a series of isolated pictures from which we draw abstract truths invested with timeless significance. We must keep reminding ourselves that the pictures we are seeing are relative to their own situation, and that they will speak properly to us only if we explore the question of response in our temporal setting in contrast with the responses the Biblical story records in that temporal setting.

The problem is intensified to some degree by the fact that the studies on which I will mainly be drawing were perhaps insufficiently conscious of this "hermeneutical circle." Before Montreal, Faith and Order studies were dominated by scholars of the so-called "Biblical theology" school. They certainly were not unaware of the work of the form critics, nor of the hermeneutical circle approach which has emerged among the post-Bultmannian scholars. But some of their "wordbook" study[8] is open to the criticism that it fails to reflect the full extent of the historical diversity of the Biblical picture. As I draw on their work, therefore, I shall attempt to correct it in this direction, but I have no doubt that here, too, the transition to a fully historical mode will be incomplete.[9]

TITLES AND IMAGES OF THE CHURCH IN THE NEW TESTAMENT

Paul Minear isolates over a hundred images of the church in the New Testament, but an analysis of the main group should be sufficient to introduce us to the various facets of the church's life which the images reveal.

1. *Ekklēsia.* This is the word that we translate as "church" in our English New Testament. It means simply, "called out." The church consists of those called out by God from among the mass of humanity to represent his purpose.

The Greek term originally denoted an assembly of people called together for a particular purpose, such as the political assemblies of the city-states. When the Old Testament was translated into Greek, *ekklēsia* was used to translate the Hebrew term *Qahal* which described Israel as the assembled people of God called out of the world to represent God's purpose among the nations. In the New Testament the followers of Christ take over the word. They see themselves as carrying on the purpose for which God called Israel out of the nations. They are now the *ekklēsia tou Kyriou* (the church of the Lord: I Cor. 2:12; Rom., ch. 16; Acts 20:28) or the *ekklēsia tou Theou* (the church of God: I Cor. 10:32; 11:22; Col. 1:18, 24; Acts 10:28). As the followers of Christ they are the representative assembly in which the nations of the world are to see their destiny. The true family relationship which is God's purpose for all has been established through their brotherhood in Christ (*adelphoi:* I Cor. 1:10).

2. *The Israel of God.* Paul rings the changes on the relationship between the nation of Israel in its calling to be God's chosen people and Christ's disciples in their continuation of God's purpose for Israel. In his allegory of the olive tree in Rom., ch. 11, continuity is clearly intended. It is the same olive tree. But the tree surgery is so radical that the extent of the discontinuity is also clear. The dead branches of the old Israel are cut out of the tree and the grafting in of the Gentiles represents a major change in the look of the tree, to say the least! Paul's point is that there is continuity here, but the continuity of God's purpose

can bring about major changes in strategy as the purpose unfolds. To interrupt the movement at any point and to make the way the church looks at that time normative for all time would be to misunderstand the mission of the church. The continuity is in Christ and his underlying purpose; the discontinuities are very considerable but can be understood within the total sweep of God's purpose.

3. *The Temple*. In the Old Testament the temple represents the place where God has chosen to dwell in the midst of his people—the place where his glory is made manifest and where the people gather to worship him. It is the place set apart as the focus point for the total relationship between God and his people.

The attitude of Jesus toward the old temple is one of radical judgment. It no longer serves to focus this relationship of living obedience to the Lord of history. (See Matt. 21:13: " 'My house shall be called a house of prayer'; but you make it a den of robbers." And Matt. 24:2: "There will not be left here one stone upon another, that will not be thrown down.") But that Jerusalem Temple with its fixed location as a separate holy place is to be replaced by a living temple which will enable disciples to celebrate God's Lordship in the context of the total human existence. When Jesus was on trial one of the charges was: "This fellow said, 'I am able to destroy the temple of God, and to build it in three days' " (Matt. 26:61). The radical change from their fixed conception was too great for them to understand. So John is forced to interpret the saying by explaining how Christ himself becomes the temple. "He spoke of the temple of his body" (John 2:21)—the body of his death and resurrection. The destruction of the old temple is final, as is the destruction of his own limited body. But the latter gives way to his resurrection presence and it is now in that presence that God dwells with his people.

This transformation of the fixed symbol is of great importance for us today. In the Christendom period the church again took on a fixed place in the world. Is its collapse a tragedy? Or does it free us to see the church in relation to the living presence of Christ within the total range of human existence? This temple symbol certainly suggests a positive answer. We have become used to the church's having fixed locations and fixed forms. How far is this expectation normative? This temple symbol as it is worked out in I Peter, where the church is likened to living stones growing up into the risen Christ, would suggest that the church has to be free to move with Christ within the structures of man's common life. Living stones are difficult for church extension architects, ecclesiastical bureaucrats, and doctrinal orthodoxists who work with fixed blueprints. Here their fixed views are called under radical question.

4. *The Body of Christ*. The symbol of the church as God's temple was radically transformed when the temple of stones was replaced by the temple of Christ's resurrection body. When Jesus died on the cross, says Matthew, the curtain of the old Temple was torn in two (Matt. 27:51). The way of God's presence is now through the sanctuary of the risen body of Jesus. The true temple is the risen Lord; the church is the body of Christ.

We are not too certain about the origins of this favorite symbol of Paul. It may be related to the Stoic use of the term "body" ("the body politic"). It is probably related to the eucharistic practice of the early Christians in which Christ made himself known to them in the breaking of the bread ("my body"). It certainly seems to indicate the faith that the risen Christ gathers his disciples to himself in such a way that they are called by him to continue in history the work of his incarnate life. They are his body for his work in the world. The profundity of this term as it draws upon the resurrection promises of Christ to the church makes it a rich store of meaning. It is no wonder that it regularly finds a central place in treatments of the doctrine of the church—particularly in Roman Catholic works, but also in all the traditions.

Nevertheless, a problem emerges in this treatment. The term has often been translated into the saying, "The church is the extension of the incarnation." The church as a visible hierarchical institution, with its head, arms, body, feet, is seen as the continuing form of Christ's presence in history. But this is a misuse of Paul's metaphor. With Paul, certainly, it carries the suggestion that the body of believers is used by Christ for his resurrection presence. But the term has a careful dialectic. There is no identity of Christ and church. Christ is the head of the body; the members have to grow up into him (Col. 1:18–20; 2:19). Baptism, putting off our flesh and rising into his resurrection body, signifies the need for a daily death (I Cor. 15:31), and the continued participation in the Lord's Supper (I Cor. 10:16–17) reminds us that our life in the body of Christ needs continual renewal.

The continuity of the visible institution as the body of Christ cannot therefore be taken for granted. There is the continuity of the promises of Christ (Word) and the continuity of the symbols of his promise (Sacraments), but the life of the church as the fellowship of believers depends upon constant renewal.[10]

5. *The Fellowship* (koinōnia). The word *koinōnia* signifies "sharers in a gift." For the early Christian church

this common gift was their life in the Spirit, given in fulfillment of the resurrection promise of Jesus.

Pentecost is often called "the birthday of the church,"
the day the Spirit was given. The Spirit must be seen as
Christ's alter ego in the church. Now that the incarnate
Christ is not visibly present among his followers, the
Spirit takes his place, incorporating the disciples into
Christ's resurrection body, distributing the gifts of Christ
(his truth, his way of life), and guiding the church in the
way of obedience to him. These gifts are not complete.
The members have to grow up into Christ as they are led
toward the final fulfillment of Christ's purpose. But they
now receive the "firstfruits" or "earnest" of this life through
the Spirit.

In the Pentecost story this new life is shown as one that
promises the final transformation of the full range of our
worldly existence. There the Spirit created a community
that broke through the barriers of language, culture, race,
sex—even possessions. Here is the promise of new life for
all the nations—a life in which the "walls of hostility"
which divide our human communities are overcome by
Christ. It is this life which is described by Paul (Gal. 3:28;
Col. 3:11) when he says that "in Christ there is no Greek
or Jew, no barbarian or Scythian, male or female, bond or
free." The church is called to be the moving sign on the
front wave of history, revealing to the nations the promise
of their destiny.

This symbol stands in constant judgment over the reality
of the empirical church! And in our day it serves as a summons for the church to risk its life on the promises of
Christ in the Spirit, seeking to reveal this new community
existence in the midst of the political and social realities
of our time. The church happens as the people of God

risk themselves upon the promises of Christ; it grows up into Christ as it receives the gifts for "edification" for the common good.

6. We have selected five of the more common terms to open up some of the rich symbolism that is used in the New Testament to point to the dimensions of the life of the church in the world. A few shorter references should be added however to indicate something more of the dynamic reality of the church's life.

The church is the *family and household of God,* sustained and disciplined by the Father through the Son, and led on by him as it is nurtured toward maturity. (John 1:12; Rom. 8:15; II Cor. 6:18; Gal. 4:5–6; I John 3:1.)

The church is the *pilgrim people,* led by God out of slavery through the wilderness of the world's life on the way to the promised land of the Kingdom, with Christ as its new Moses or expedition leader (*archēgos*). (Heb. 2:10; I Peter 2:9–11; Titus 2:11–14; Heb. 8:8–13.) As a pilgrim people the church has to lead a relatively rootless existence (in tents) so that it can be free to move on with Christ as he fights his way through history to the completed Kingdom.

In these terms we catch something of the reality of the church as the visible servant of God's purpose, called to be the body through which the risen Christ reveals the shape of the new Kingdom in which the restrictive limits of the world's communities are broken through, and standing constantly under the call of Christ to be ready for new forms of obedience.

It is interesting to compare the characteristics here with the traditional catalog of the "notes" of the church embodied in the creeds. The church is:

One. All the terms we have analyzed presuppose unity.

The church is the sign of the ultimate unity of all things in Christ. Believers are growing up into "one new man," and their growing unity is the promise of final unity for the creation.

Holy. Holiness is a status given to the chosen community because it is set apart by God for his service. But the holiness of the church in the New Testament is eschatological: It is set apart as a sign of God's purpose to fill all creation with his presence, and it must grow up into the life of holiness. Holiness is no longer the cultic quality of a special place in life, but a gift to the church in the midst of life. This gift is also a mission: The church is called to be a sign of God's intention that this gift is for all creation.

Catholic. This points in tradition to both the wholeness of the church's life—the fullness of the truth it has received—and the wholeness of its mission—it exists for all the world and so transcends the narrow boundaries of all smaller communities. The New Testament images we have explored certainly confirm these meanings of the term. But it is clear that "Catholic" must be understood historically—as a mission given to the church—rather than ontologically—in the sense of a status guaranteed to an institution. Catholicity is a gift of the Spirit, but it is a gift that has to be appropriated; it has to happen. The church is catholic as it reveals how Christ is drawing the world out of its brokenness.

Apostolic. The apostles were chosen by Christ to be his authoritative witnesses, and the church continues this primary apostolic task of witness to him. Within this term, however, there is concealed a major historical problem. Is there a particular unbroken institutional line of continuity with the apostles—through Peter as primate to his successors in Rome and/or through the Twelve to their

E

successors, the bishops? Or is the term "apostolic" satisfied by the continuation of the faithful witness begun by the apostles and carried on by the church through forms of order which can be properly varied according to different political and social situations in which the witness occurs?

This vexing question calls for an analysis of the Biblical record and an assessment of the present problem of the church in the light of the conflicting traditions.

APOSTOLIC SUCCESSION

The choice of the Twelve by Christ and the symbolic use made of this in the New Testament point to the continuity of the church with the twelve tribes of Israel. The apostles are significant also, not only because they are chosen by Jesus as the representative group of witnesses during his life, but because they are sealed in that authority after his death by being the major witnesses of his resurrection. After the defection of Judas his place is filled, so that at the final scene of the central redemptive drama—Pentecost—the church is launched out from Jerusalem with its foundations complete.

But what is the apostles' continuing significance? It could be argued from the New Testament that there is none. The foundation is now laid and this particular apostolic symbolism is therefore complete. The twelve symbolism disappears, and the term "apostle" becomes varied. Paul is beyond the structure of the Twelve, as one "born out of due time" to be the "apostle to the Gentiles." Here at last the radical newness of the mission of the church is revealed and its freedom from the limiting institutions of the old Israel—temple, circumcision, cultic laws. The institutional swaddling clothes are thrown off—the first stage of Israel's mission is completed and past.

It can be argued, in reply, that the use of the term "apostle" for Paul does not reduce the need for continuing visible unity with the apostles in institutional historical succession. The inclusion of Paul simply emphasizes the new phase into which the apostolic witness must enter. Paul himself recognizes the need for a special intervention by Christ to add him to the authorized witnesses, and he takes pains to check his credentials with Peter and the Jerusalem brethren.

There are, however, further difficulties. James the brother of Jesus is also spoken of as an apostle, as are Barnabas, Junias, and Andronicus. What can be made of these? Adolf Schlatter argues that the appointment of James the brother of Jesus as a pillar apostle in Jerusalem means that the church respected the natural order—the descent within the Jewish family of David. James was chosen to represent God's continuing faithfulness to the old Israel (Jewish Christianity), in the same way that Paul was called to symbolize God's new work beyond Israel among the Gentiles.

But what of Barnabas, Junias, and Andronicus? It has been argued by "Catholic" apologists that this is a secondary use of apostles.[11] These are "church apostles" appointed by the church to particular missions in distinction from "Christ's apostles" who were appointed by him as the authorized witnesses of his life, death, and resurrection. It must be confessed, however, that such arguments are simply means by which the imprecise language of the New Testament is ordered to agree with the later views of the early Catholic church.

What then are we to conclude? My present view is that the foundation function of the Twelve was complete with them. For that apostolic function no succession is required.

But the church did care about orderly historic continuity. Paul did go to Jerusalem to keep visible unity. As the early church subsequently faced the problems of order and unity it used the symbol of apostolic continuity in a new way by choosing a particular order—episcopal—to be a visible symbol of the unity of faith and life. That symbol has been effectively used through much of the church's history—the symbol of the continuity of the church's purpose and witness across time and space. But it has also at times been misused, and this was the reason for the Reformation revolt in the name of the apostles' faith against those who claimed to be the apostles' successors. Here we see the reason for the assertion of the vertical view of ecclesiology over against the horizontal.

Facing both of these historical facts, we are forced to make decisions about them in actual church union schemes. My belief is that we can value the symbol of apostolic succession—an episcopal line with visible continuity reaching out across space and back through time to the age of the apostles—as a valuable symbol of the unity of the church. But equally we must insist that such a continuity is no guarantee of faithfulness, and that the clear use of the other traditions by Christ for his apostolic witness must be confessed and recognized in the church's order.

A similar analysis of Peter's place of priority seems justified. In every list of apostles his name is first. In every key situation (Caesarea Philippi, transfiguration, Mount of Olives, Gethsemane), Peter is always in the small group separated from the rest and consistently acts as the spokesman. And it now seems clear that in Matt. 16:18–19 the words of Jesus giving to Peter the place of the rock and the gift of the keys must be taken as the recognition of a place of doctrinal and disciplinary authority in the community. Peter is the primary spokesman of the community to the world, and he exercised that function after Pentecost.

What are we to say then? That the church was given a primate and that the tradition of Peter's successor in Rome has solid roots in the Biblical story? It is not as simple as that. Peter's foundation role seems to be in the main complete after Pentecost. Paul then exercises authority in his area; James, in Jerusalem. When Paul challenges Peter's attitude over Jew–Gentile relationships the question is decided by a council (Acts, ch. 15). Similarly in John's Gospel (ch. 20:23) the apostolic authority given to Peter in Matthew is given to the whole community. The later hierarchical structure of Rome is obviously not authorized here.

However, our answer cannot be a simple no to the primacy tradition. The New Testament does take the visible institutional unity of the church seriously as an essential aspect of the church's witness among the institutions of the world. The representation of that unity under the Peter figure was then used by the church in an attempt to accomplish what the Roman Empire through its caesars had failed to do. We may now judge it as a glorious attempt which ultimately failed because it took over too easily the world's structures of power. The authority Peter exercised was a servant authority and was one that was shared with the whole body. Now the Roman Church is undertaking a painful reassessment of its authoritarian order. The authority of the laity is being gradually rediscovered along with the servant character of true authority.

But is there no value in personal expressions of the apostolic mission and of the unity of life in Christ in bishops, and even in one bishop symbolically representing all? The unity of the mission has its personal center in Jesus Christ, and personal expressions of that mission and of the unity of that mission are consistent with the New Testament understanding of the church's presence in the world.

CHAPTER IV

A Dogmatic Approach—
The Christological Analogy

Several of the New Testament images remind us how closely the community of believers identified their corporate life with Christ. The church is the body of Christ; it is the bride of Christ; the resurrection Christ is now the temple of God with believers as living stones growing up into him.

It was inevitable that theologians would turn to Christology—the formulated expression of the person and work of Christ—expecting to find clues to help them grasp the nature and work of the church. The Faith and Order movement turned in this direction at its meeting in Lund in 1952. We have already seen, however, that we must be careful to observe here the difference as well as the similarity in using the analogy of Christ as a guide to the life of the church. We must not simply identify them in simple continuity, with the church's being seen as "the extension of the incarnation." Christ retains his difference from the church as its head—its guide who rules it by his judgment and grace. The members of the church are members of Christ's body only through the continued death of repentance and resurrection by his promise. They are forgiven sinners growing up into him.

Our use of the Christological analogy, therefore, works from the truth that Christ identifies with the church as his body, but it is limited by the awareness that the church is not identified as Christ. Its life is dependent upon Christ in the same way that the life of the believer is dependent on Christ. It lives by "justification," its imperfect life having the status of Christ's body only through the forgiveness of Christ by which it participates in his righteousness. Living under this justification, it therefore also lives under the promise that it can grow up into Christ. As traditional theology put it, Christ's new life is not only "imputed" to it, but it is also "imparted" so that it is able to begin showing forth the fruits of this new life. In that way the church is enabled to be the sign of the world's destiny. For it is God's purpose that the whole creation shall grow up into Christ.

Because it is created by Christ to be the form of his continuing presence in the world, the church has a reality that is greater than the life of the individual believer. Believers are brought to life through and in the church where they grow up into Christ. This priority of the church in relation to the believer reflects Christ's purpose that each of us shall find our true destiny only in relation to one another and to the creation. It is to the church that Christ grants "the means of grace." The church has received his Word (and the witness to it in Scripture) and his ordinances (his symbolic rites through which he enables the believers to grow into his corporate life in the dramatic reenactment of his redeeming way). It is to the church also that he gives his task of discipling: "Go ye."

Here we see the significance of the Christological teaching that Christ is not simply an individual man but the corporate man. And here is the truth behind the teaching of the fathers (and the Reformers) that the church is our "mother," for it is only in and through the church that we are brought to life.

It is from this, too, that the persistent teaching derives: *Extra ecclesiam nulla salus* ("Outside the church no salvation"). This saying is important in the sense that Christ gives us true life in and with his corporate life. Where it is questionable is where it is assumed that a continuously visible community is "the church," outside of which Christ's community and his saving life do not exist. That limited view has been rejected now by Rome. The source of its error is that it identifies Christ too closely with the visible church, forgetting that the community exists by justification alone and that Christ is free to bypass the particular community in judgment, bringing forth the signs of his new life beyond its limits. In I Peter 4:17 we are reminded that "judgment must begin at the house of God," and in Rev., chs. 2 and 3, it is the churches (not just individuals in them) that are addressed with the call to repentance and are warned that unless they repent, Christ will spew them out of his mouth.

We can say therefore:

1. That because Christ identifies himself so closely with his church, giving it his gifts of grace as the promise of his presence, like him (to use the analogy of Christological doctrine) it is divine and human. It is divine in the sense that it is the God-elected sign of the divine purpose and the God-chosen instrument of his witness and service. It is human in the sense that it has all the characteristics of other human institutions and must live in the world in the same way in which they live in the world. As a divine community, however, it exists to reveal God's true purpose for all human communities. It is the "eschatological com-

munity" in the same way that Christ is the "eschatological man"—the sign of the end or goal.

This eschatological task of the church is made clear in the Pentecost story. Just as in Jesus of Nazareth we are given in one man the perfect picture of God's intended life for every man—he is the new Adam—so at Pentecost we are given at one point in history the perfect miniature picture of God's intended life-in-community. There a new community is created in Christ in which all the barriers that stand in the way of true community are broken down. The church is created in its pristine moment as the "bride of Christ," the body of Christ, the sign of the "one new Man."[1]

2. That because the humanity of the church is not the sinlessness of Christ's humanity, it lives as a "justified" community, supported by his faithfulness but subject to his judgment. The eschatalogical task of being the sign of the world's destiny as the new community in Christ in which all the barriers to true community are taken down can be so forgotten by the church in its acquiescence in race, class, and caste separations that it ceases to be the sign of the new humanity in Christ. What then? Does this mean that the visible institution is constantly falling into faithlessness and constantly being bypassed as God ever and again acts to bring forth the event of the church—the true sign of Christ's purpose for the "new humanity"—in unexpected places?

We are tempted to answer yes to this. For surely this bypassing has had to occur in various reformations, and there is no reason to expect that the story will not be repeated. But this is an eventuality caused by our faithlessness. Christ still works in his faithfulness to restore unity to his divided church so that it may be more effective in its mission. Even when he bypasses it so that the mission for which the church is created may continue, still he remains faithful and works to restore the visible unity of his body as the sign of the ultimate unity of creation in him.

It is this lack of dialectic in his ecclesiology which betrays Brunner in his *Misunderstanding of the Church*.[2] Brunner rightly rejects the view that the continuity of true life in Christ has been guaranteed to a visible institution whose limits are guarded by a given priesthood with authority over the mission of Christ in the world. The sinful institution can become so much a barrier to the true life and witness of Christ that Christ bypasses it. But from there Brunner makes a great jump. Because the institution *must* always be sinful, therefore it can never be the true ecclesia. "The New Testament *Ecclesia,* the fellowship of Jesus Christ, is a pure communion of persons and has nothing of the character of an institution about it."[3]

Here we cannot follow him. The human character of the church must include "incarnation" in the institutional life of the world. This includes the important calling to be a sign of the true community in Christ. The sinful character of the community, with its life being always an existence as a justified sinner—*simul iustus et peccator*—means that it serves as that sign only as it struggles against the tendency to be drawn down to the limits of the other communities of the world. The possibility always exists that the institution may be brought under God's judgment and bypassed. But it is again an institution that emerges to carry on the witness.

In the story in The Acts we are given a striking description of the church's self-understanding in this initial moment of its history. "They devoted themselves to the apostles' teaching and fellowship, to the breaking of bread and the prayers." (Acts 2:42.) Included in this statement are three institutional characteristics: (*a*) The church depends for its being upon *the apostolic message;* (*b*) the church continues as *an apostolic fellowship;* (*c*) the church centers its life around *a particular form of cultus.*

1. The church depends for its existence on *the apostolic message.* It is for this reason that the New Testament emerged as an institutional expression—a canon or measure—of the apostolic understanding of the meaning of the coming of Christ in history for the redemption of the world. Paul's statement, "I traditioned [delivered] unto you that which was traditioned unto me," is an expression of this truth that the church exists through this given apostolic witness to Christ (I Cor. 15:3).

The form in which this apostolic message should receive institutional expression was (and is) a difficult question. The need for a given form with an approved summary of the apostolic message was already expressed in the "early Catholicism" of the pastoral epistles. "Follow the pattern of the sound words which you have heard from me, in the faith and love which are in Christ Jesus; guard the truth that has been entrusted to you by the Holy Spirit who dwells within us." (II Tim. 1:13–14.) The extensive witness to the apostolic witness which was being collected into the New Testament was not adequately self-interpreting to provide the church with a confessional sense of its common faith in Christ. An intensive interpretative summary was needed—a need that gave rise to the Apostles' Creed.

With these developments, however, there was a growing danger that such objective measures of the church's continuity with the apostolic faith would withdraw attention from the repetition of apostolic faith which was the true continuity and to which objective standards could only point. The need for the *horizontal,* visible continuity of witness to intersect with the *vertical,* the event of faith to which the witness points, is recognized in the statement in II Timothy: The pattern of sound words can be followed only "in the faith and love which are in Christ Jesus"; the truth entrusted can be guarded only "by the Holy Spirit who dwells within us." Horizontal continuity is indispensable, for there is a story with a definite pattern that has to be told; but the vertical event is the point of the story. The difficulty is that there is no guarantee that the intersection will occur.

2. The church depends for its continuation on the maintenance of *the apostolic fellowship.* Did this include continuing in a fellowship over which the apostles and their successors were given authority? Probably there was some such assumption: that the church had to have clear order and provision for orderly succession, and that Christ's choice of the Twelve indicated the need to continue such orderly structures in the community of the faithful. But this does not mean that the early church assumed that *a* particular order was necessary. In fact there seems good evidence that there was real freedom in relating the order to particular political and social circumstances of that time.[4] It was only when there was considerable growth in numbers that a need was felt to develop *one* uniform order, with a monarchical episcopate finally emerging with authority over the apostolic message and cultus.

A further and more important aspect of apostolic fellowship seems evident. We have seen how the Pentecost story centers on the creation of a fellowship in which the barriers of race, language, and culture fell beneath the powerful awareness of a new unity in Christ given them by the Spirit. This fellowship was the climactic act of the redemp-

tive drama to which the apostles were witness. The fellowship in which they shared was a gift offered to the broken
communities of the earth.

Here again we see the tension between the *horizontal*—
apostolic order with its visible continuity—and the *vertical*
—the event in which the Spirit creates a fellowship that
breaks through the limits of our ordinary human communities. There was both continuity with Israel and
discontinuity occasioned by the radical newness of the in-
clusive fellowship created by the Spirit. The tension continued to have profound meaning in the early Christian
community, just as it has profound meaning still. If one
side is followed in forgetfulness of the other, serious distortion can occur.

We can illustrate this through the interpretation of the
saying of Cyprian to which we have already referred: *Extra
ecclesiam nulla salus*. When this is interpreted in a horizontal and juridical sense and the question becomes, Is it
possible for anyone to be saved outside the community
ruled by the successors of Peter and the apostles? then the
statement leads to an obviously awkward conclusion! The
Roman Catholic Church for a long time gave the answer
that there is no ordinary chance of salvation outside that
community. But recognizing the difficulties, they had to
say that there are "uncovenanted mercies"—which is to
say, surely, that it is fortunate that God's mercy has broader
boundaries than our legalistic theologies! If the phrase,
on the other hand, were interpreted simply in the vertical
sense, the effect would be no better. It would simply say
that wherever a true community event occurs, there is the
church (i.e., the true community!) and salvation.

The apostolic faith to which the church witnesses, and
for which the order of the church was created, carries in it

the promise of an apostolic community. The former (the witness) is given to point to the latter (the community), and the church is meant to be the community of salvation. But it is possible that the church with impeccable credentials of horizontal continuity may come to stand in the way of the vertical event of apostolic community. Then it is no longer truly the church, for there is no longer evidenced within it the life of salvation—the redeemed life of the new community.

A recent World Council of Churches' study on "The Holy Spirit and the Catholicity of the Church," in exploring the problem of the continuity of the church in relation to the obvious breaks in continuity, relates this tension to God's mercy and judgment:

This awareness of the twofold dealing of God with men, in mercy and in judgment, may provide a clue to the understanding of true and false continuity within the church. . . . True continuity is safeguarded by breaking false traditions. . . . *The true continuity is in his work of judgment as well as mercy. . . .*

Even in time of division, however, the Holy Spirit does not cease working in the divided churches, just as under the Old Covenant after the division of the Northern and the Southern Kingdom. God raised prophets in both. Therefore the Church does not cease to confess its faith in the one church. She knows that God's faithfulness and promise is finally the ground of unity.[5]

3. The church centers its life around *a particular cultus* —"the breaking of bread and the prayers." The early Christians, like their Lord, "day by day went to the temple." The cultus of Israel was cleansed by Christ, but its intention was continued. Christ submitted to baptism as the external initiatory sign of the penitent community and gave baptism as the sign of entrance for all believers.

He instituted a new rite on Maundy Thursday in line with the old Passover but transformed it by his final sacrifice, and (as other rabbis did) he taught prayers to his community within the framework of his own redeeming work.

This cultus was the visible sign of his community; its rites were dramatic signs pointing to the vertical reenactment in the life of the community of his saving work. They carried with them the promise that he would preside at the reenactment.

In this sign we see the same tension between the *horizontal*—the continuation of the given cult—and the *vertical*—the entrance into the reality to which the cult points. Again there is no guarantee that where one is, there will the other be also.

We see in these three institutional characteristics the basis for "the marks of the church" theology of the Reformers: "The church is where the Word is truly preached and the Sacraments duly administered." As we have argued, there is a real meaning in this emphasis, but it is the lack of adequate recognition of the event character of the church that tends to turn it into a legalistic measuring rod which prevents the real question's being asked. That is why (as we noticed in Chapter I) "mission" was first added to these marks in ecumenical discussions, leading later to the more radical insistence that the event character of the church must be given primacy. The horizontal factors are instrumental—they are at the service of the event. The church is, first of all, the happening of Christ's continuing presence in his community and, through it, in the world.

But our analysis has led us to see a danger from the other side if the event ecclesiology is pushed too far. The community of the church is always imperfect—so that the event itself is one in which a very imperfect obedience is

accepted within the gracious forgiveness of Christ. That
is why so many terms for the church in the New Testament
center on the growing that the community of the church
still has to do:

a. The church is the bride still being prepared for pres-
entation to Christ (II Cor. 11:2).

b. It is in process of growing up into Christ (Col. 1:18–
20; 2:19).

c. It is the pilgrim people still under training and moving toward the Promised Land under its expedition leader
(Heb. 2:10).

The horizontal signs—the given Word, Sacraments, ministry—point to Christ's continuing faithfulness in the midst
of our unfaithfulness. But the question is, At what point
does our faithlessness lead to judgment and to Christ's
bypassing of the community he has created?

This is the question dealt with in Rev., chs. 19 to 21.
There the church is seen as Christ's engaged. bride constantly in danger of becoming a harlot. Before the church
is ready for the marriage supper of the Lamb it must participate in the creation of the new heaven and the earth.
The church shares in the agony of creation, waiting for
its final redemption in Christ; but its deeper agony lies in
its mission of revealing to the creation the direction of its
destiny. Will she be judged unworthy of this task and bypassed?

The seven churches are passed in review. *Ephesus* is
faithful in some things, but still must repent for not showing the great love it had at first. *Smyrna* is in the clear, but
Pergamum is called to account for not guarding the truth
sufficiently against Balaamites and Nicolaitans, and *Thya-
tira* is in danger for tolerating the false prophetess Jezebel.
With *Sardis* the case is even worse, for its failure of obedi-

F

ence makes it of doubtful use. *Philadelphia* is faithful, but *Laodicea*'s lukewarmness is such that it is in danger of being spewed out of Christ's mouth.

What if they should not repent? Will Christ bypass them and raise up other children unto Abraham? That seemed to be the case at the time of the Reformers. Luther and Calvin agreed that the true church could still be found within the old structures, but they believed that they were called by Christ to raise the banner of his word afresh so that Christ could call his faithful community into clearer visibility. But their question was, How do we know that the point of tolerated faithlessness which justifies the breach of horizontal continuity and visible unity has been reached? There is no assured answer.

Claude Welch puts the dilemma of the church as follows:

(1) How can this divided, faltering, sinful company be rightfully called a new creation, the bride cleansed, the community of the justified, the way of salvation, the first-fruits of the new age, the temple of the *Holy* Spirit? (2) How can this association of men, conformable apparently to the patterns of a multitude of other human associations, be rightfully described as the people *of* God, the colony *of heaven,* the *royal* priesthood, *God's* planting, the body of *Christ?*[6]

The answer is not simply to acquiesce in the wheat and the tares growing up together. In the New Testament there was no such pleading of the inevitability of the sinfulness of the church's existence as a reason for failure to be the sign of Christ's purpose for his world. Instead, there is a constant struggle against its sinfulness with a constant reminder that daily repentance includes reaching out to the new community life of Christ. The people of God make no attempt to hide their weaknesses. They participate in fact in the full reality of the world Christ is struggling to redeem. But they know that Christ is struggling with them also to make them the instruments of his purpose.

All this means that it is the fully human existence of the church that is the raw material Christ uses as the sign of his power to redeem the world. Its life is expected to reveal certain characteristics that will distinguish it from other human communities. For while it is a truly human institution reflecting the sinful weaknesses of its members, it is also "the people of God," called into the renewing process of Christ through the Spirit.

For this reason there must be a vertical dependence upon God which can reveal that the church lives by response to the gracious act of God. It must be loyal to the truth by which it lives and must guard the deposit of faith, allowing its life to be constantly reformable under that gospel. The canon of Scripture, the interpretative guide of the creeds, the teaching office in the church— these are gifts of Christ to help preserve the witness. But still there is no guarantee that these external aids will mean that the community is abiding in the truth. That is an event promised to faith, and the church constantly faces the question, When the Son of Man comes shall he find faith on the earth?

The truth into which the church is called and of which it is to be the sign is the truth of the new life in Christ. "By this we may be sure that we know him, if we keep his commandments." (I John 2:3.) A believer who departs from the way and who refuses to hear the correcting word may be disciplined by excommunication, but with the knowledge that Christ's word to him still stands and that the way to unity with him through repentance is still open (Matt. 18:15).

So it is with the community. It is called by Christ to the service of the word, and called to carry forward the mission of Christ by revealing his servant form (Phil., ch. 2). It is called out in order to be sent forth. "You are a chosen race, . . . that you may declare the wonderful deeds of him who called you out of darkness into his marvelous light." (I Peter 2:9.) But if the salt has lost its savor, if the branches of the vine are not bearing fruit, Christ may bypass the savorless, fruitless community, although the sign of his prior faithfulness to his broken church remains. He longs to restore its faithfulness and heal its brokenness "that the world may know" (John 17:23).

Chapter V

The Time of the Church's Mission

In the Old Testament the Sabbath is the sacred day among the secular days—the day set apart for unbroken meditation on God's purpose and his law, the day which could be so penetrated by God's presence that it could serve as a foretaste of the Messianic age when all time would be transparent to the way of God. And if the Sabbath was that representative piece of time which served as a sign of God's purpose for all time, the temple was the representative piece of space which served as the sign of God's purpose for all space.

In the New Testament the concept of the Sabbath became problematic. Now that Christ had come, and now that his risen presence was continuously with the world, the distinction between the sacred and the secular began to disintegrate. There was no longer a temple made with hands which served as a focus center for God's presence: Christ, the temple not made with hands, was available in all space. There was no longer a sacred day when one point of time served as a sign of the ultimate penetration of all time. Now the Messiah had come—"And lo, I am with you always, to the close of the age" (Matt. 28:20).

It was not that all time and space had now been filled

with God's ultimate purpose for it. That fulfillment was only in one man—Jesus Christ. But he was now available to all times and places. In him the world's true destiny had come. The world, however, still has to enter into this inheritance. And that is where the church comes in. This time between the time when the Messianic age is inaugurated by Christ and the time when the world will finally receive the full inheritance is the time of the church's mission. In this sense the whole of this time is church time.

Two recorded sayings of Jesus in Matthew's Gospel spell this out:

1. "This gospel of the kingdom will be preached throughout the whole world as a testimony to all nations and then the end will come." (Matt. 24:14.)

This period of history is given so that all nations will have the opportunity to hear the gospel. It is the time given for the church to take the gospel of Christ to all the world, and for those who hear the story to learn the way of Christ and to begin practicing it. It is the time for the church through word and deeds to penetrate the life of the world with the love of Christ and so to call the world to its destiny.

2. "Go therefore and make disciples of all nations, baptizing them in the name of the Father and of the Son and of the Holy Spirit." (Matt. 28:19.)

The command is given to the church to go to all nations and to draw them into the way of discipleship with Christ. It is not just time given to the church to tell the story. It is time for the hearers to have a chance to learn the way of Christ and to be gathered into the life of the new community through baptism. But it does not end with the church. The command continues: "teaching them to observe all that I have commanded you." There is time for the new community to practice this way of Christ in such a manner as to penetrate the life of the world.

Church time, therefore, is now also world time. It is time for the church to point the world to its true destiny. In this time, Christ is not present visibly. The church has been given the task of interpreting his hidden presence to the world. But when this stage of history is completed, the nations of the world shall then walk directly in his light, and the church's day will be over. The seer in catching a vision of the final Kingdom "saw no temple therein" (Rev. 21:22). The church will have withered away; there will be no need for its mediating service.

In this present time, the task of the church is two-dimensional. It must move out—into all the world. But it also has a depth task: life has to be penetrated with Christ's purpose. This does not mean that the church has to draw all the world under its institutional sway, and move toward a time when the church shall be all in all. Instead, the church points beyond itself to the time when Christ shall be all in all. The church, as a separate institution, points to the purpose of Christ for all the institutions of life. It seeks to serve those institutions in such a way that they will be called to their true purpose.[1]

This vision is spelled out in the letters to the Colossians and the Ephesians. Colossians, for example, speaks of the community of the church as the place in which the new life in Christ is appearing in the world. In the life of the church the world should see what it is to become. (Col., chs. 2; 3.) But this new life, received in the church, is meant to penetrate the structures of the world. For that reason, the community of the church with Christ as the head is the sign of the final outcome of history in which the whole creation will have Christ as its head (ch. 1:15–

20). Paul speaks of the church as already planted in the whole world and bearing fruit and growing (v. 6). That certainly did not mean that there was a church in every village! Rather, it reflected his belief that when the church was planted at all the crucial crossroads—and that was his strategy—then the life of Christ would be able to penetrate all the structures of the world. The church as an institution does not need to fill the whole world. The church is a representative community—*pars pro toto* ("a part on behalf of the whole"). In this community God's purpose is revealed for the whole community, and the church serves to channel Christ's servant way into all the structures of life.

This servant role of the church is modeled on the way of its Lord. "The servant shall not be above the master." He exercised his Lordship by humbling himself in the role of a servant. As Paul states it in Phil., ch. 2, it was precisely because he took upon himself the form of a servant and identified himself with the conditions of our needy humanity that God exalted him as Lord. It was to serve, to minister, that he came. In that service he revealed the way through which God is working out his purpose for the world. In the Servant the world will at last acknowledge its Lord.

Karl Barth describes the coming of Christ as "The Way of the Son of God Into the Far Country."[2] The Lordship of Christ is exhibited in his identification with us in our lostness, our sinfulness, our disobedience. It is in that servant identification that his omnipotence and glory are disclosed. His greatest glory is in his stooping. His omnipotence is in the love that serves and condescends to be identified with man in his suffering and need. In Christ humiliation and servant love are seen as the essence of deity. God is God in his being for man in history.

True, Christ is not imprisoned within the limits of our history. In his resurrection he breaks through the present limits of our conditions and points to the transformation of creation and the opening of history to the ultimate fulfillment of God's purpose for man. But the way to this transformation is the way of the servant, and the church is called to witness to that way. So in Phil., ch. 2, the Christian community is summoned to "let this mind be in you, which was also in Christ Jesus." The servant way of Christ is the divine mode for bringing the world under the rule of God.

Christ entered fully into our human situation. "He learned obedience through what he suffered" (Heb. 5:8), and in his wrestling for man in the particular situation of that time, he showed the way the church is called to follow. Paul trod that way and believed that by following this path the church is fulfilling Christ's saving purpose. "I, Paul, . . . fill up what is lacking in the afflictions of Christ, on behalf of his body, the church." (Col. 1:24.)

In the fulfillment of this ministry the church has two roles to play. In its own internal life it practices the servant way in such a fashion that its community life becomes an illustration of the new way. "Bear one another's burdens and so fulfil the law of Christ." (Gal. 6:2.) Externally, within the structures of the world, the church is also called to take the servant presence of its Lord. This is made clear in the letter to the Ephesians. The first part of the letter tells how the life of Christ has removed the veil that had kept the secret of God's purpose for history hidden. In Christ, God has shown that it is his purpose to gather all things in heaven and earth alike into unity in Christ. The second part of the letter then spells out the practical meaning of this for the life of the church. The description begins with what this means for the church as a separate institution. (Eph. ch. 4.) The quality of the life of the new community must reveal the true nature of life in Christ. But that is followed in the subsequent chapters by a description of how this "walk in love" is to work its way out into the institutions of the world—into the family (ch. 5:22 ff.) and into master-slave relationships (ch. 6:5 ff.).

In Chapter I we described an important contemporary difference of emphasis concerning the roles of the church. Balthasar emphasized the role of the church as a separate institution showing in its own life the signs of God's purpose for all life. The church is called first to be a city set on a hill. Hoekendijk stressed the need for the church to point away from its own institutional life to the places where Christ is working out his purpose in the struggles for true human life within the other institutions of the world. The church needs its separate life—house churches in which believers are trained for their servant role in the world. But this life must be humble and unobtrusive, with the church community making itself available to Christ in his struggle for true community within the structures of the world. The church is called to be leaven in the world.

Perhaps the Ephesians letter gives us a clue as to how to handle this vital difference. In the early church situation the Balthasar emphasis was primary. The life of the church itself was a sign that a new community life is available: that it is possible for conflicts of race, culture, class, and sex to be overcome and for a fellowship to emerge beyond the death of these ancient hostilities. At that time, penetration of the structures of the world was limited, but nonetheless important. Christians had major access to family life, and they made the most of that opportunity to show how the servant way of Christ could transform it. They had a limited access to the master-slave relationship—not enough at that time to break through the massive institution of slavery, but enough to begin to transform the superiority assumptions that lay behind it. In those days, then, the city-set-on-a-hill role was predominant. But later as the church grew, so its access to the other institutions increased. As a result the leaven role became increasingly important.

What then is the relation between the two roles today? Both are still vital, but in different situations the balance may vary considerably. In some countries the church is in a situation similar to that of the first century, with little access to the other institutions. But in others it has considerable opportunity to join Christ in his struggle for a truly human existence within the institutions of the world. Then, Hoekendijk rightly insists, it must train its members to fulfill that servant role in the world, humbly pointing away from its own life to those places on the frontiers of life where the key struggles for human community are going on. This does not mean that the role of the church as a city set on a hill disappears. There is still need for the church to seek to serve Christ as a demonstration community, where the way of the future is being tested. But what the extent of this separate life should be and how far the church should go in seeking to disperse that life of demonstration of the servant way into the other institutions—these are points where real differences of judgment will continue to exist.

Here we cannot expect any direct guidance from the New Testament. In the New Testament the treatment of the institutions of the world is rather stylized. There is a rather formal description of what were later called the "orders." The family, the economic order, and the state were the three God-given institutions with which the church had to be concerned. The church was the institution through which God's purpose for life was becoming visible. Meanwhile, the other three institutions were used by God to keep the world in order, until the way of life now becoming visible in the church could penetrate all the institutions and bring them to the direct acceptance of the rule of their Lord.

This formalized description of the orders was an accurate enough reflection of the life of rural society—a life that was dominant through the centuries right down to our time. But now we are in a rapidly changing situation. The rise of the urban society is introducing a much more complicated institutional pattern for human existence. It is necessary now to redefine the Biblical picture of the relations of the church as an institution to the institutions of the world.

Bonhoeffer speaks of the way in which the acceptance by Jesus of the institutions of marriage, labor, and government leads to their recognition as "divine mandates."[3] Jesus blessed marriage by his participation in the life of a family and by "his first miracle which he wrought in Cana of Galilee"; he blessed labor by his years as a carpenter; he blessed government by accepting its authority over him even at the moment of its greatest sin. From these relationships, Jesus made it clear that these mandates are essential to God's way of ruling the world.

Take government or the state as an example.[4] The attitude of Jesus to the state is reflected in some typical texts:

John 19:1–11. "You would have no power over me, unless it had been given you from above." The authority government exercises is intended by God, and for that reason Jesus respects it. Because that power is so often misused government has to be recalled to its true purpose, but Jesus does not correct that misuse by an external imposition of higher power. He seeks to redeem it from within by his servant love—even when that servant way leads to suffering at the state's hands.

Mark 12:13–17. The Pharisees ask Jesus: "Is it lawful to pay taxes to Caesar, or not?" In reply Jesus asks his questioners for a coin. They produce it, and on it are shown the images of Caesar. Their use of the coin is a tacit recognition that they cannot live without participating in the economic and legal order maintained by Caesar. That leads to a rejection of the view of the Pharisees and Herodians that Caesar, as an instrument of foreign domination, is without divine authority. "Render to Caesar the things that are Caesar's." It is right to pay taxes to Caesar, for they are essential to the state's God-given role of keeping justice, order, and peace.

But Jesus does not stop there. He continues: Render "to God the things that are God's." There is a limit to subservience to the state. Since the purposes of God have ultimate authority, the state must be denied the right to absolute obedience—to worship.

This cryptic saying of Jesus, with its explosive inner tensions, is reflected in the attitude of the church to the state in the rest of the New Testament.

1. The mandate of the state is affirmed—the positive teaching (e.g., Rom. 13:1 ff.; I Peter 2:13–17; I Tim. 2:1–3).

Christians are taught to accept the authority of government as God-given, and in the New Testament there is a strong "ethics of submission," undoubtedly inspired by Christ's attitude ·of humble obedience. Paul, in Rom., ch. 13, calls state authorities God's servants, "instituted by

God." Their servant role or ministry is given them by
God. They have the task of putting down wrongdoing
and maintaining order and justice, and Christians are to
affirm that God-given role by a positive attitude of obedience. The same theme is strongly expressed in I Peter,
ch. 2, where Christians are told to set an example by their
obedience.

In I Tim., ch. 2, this attitude of the church's responsibility to the state is taken even farther. "I urge that sup-
plications, prayers, intercessions, and thanksgivings be
made for all men, for kings and all who are in high posi-
tions, that we may lead a quiet and peaceable life, godly
and respectful in every way." (Vs. 1–2.) The church has
a liturgical responsibility for the world—and particularly
for the state. It must seek to draw the state toward the true
fulfillment of its God-given role by its liturgical witness to
the proper place of the state in the mission of God.

That place is spelled out in the following verse: "This is
good, and it is acceptable in the sight of God our Savior,
who desires all men to be saved and to come to the knowledge of the truth." Here the partnership between the
church and the other institutions in the working out of
God's purpose is clearly recognized. The order kept by
the state makes possible the quiet, peaceful, godly life to
which the church is summoning the world. If all men are
to hear about Christ's way and are to accept it and practice it, then the government's work of maintaining order
must be seen as an essential precondition.

This positive understanding of the role of government
(and of the other institutions) gives us a basis for the strong
contemporary emphasis on the "secular obedience" of
Christians and on the need for the church to train the
laity for their role as servants within the structures of the

world. But in the attempt to assess the importance of this positive understanding of the secular structures as the places of mission, further guidance is provided by the story of the temptations of Jesus (e.g., Luke 4:1–12). In these, the relation of the mission of Jesus to the economic order and to the state are at the heart of the struggle.

Temptation 1: "Command this stone that it be made bread." Jesus is tempted to use his power to intervene in the economic order in such a way as to impose God's purpose upon it. He rejects this as contrary to God's way. The way to release the capacities of God's creation so that human needs will be met has to be learned from within. And if man is to unlock those secrets so that the economic order can fulfill God's purpose, this will require unlocking also the deeper secrets of love and compassion. "Man shall not live by bread alone." It is as man learns to live the servant way that he will also learn the true use of the economic order.

Temptation 2: Christ is offered all the kingdoms of the world with their authority and glory if he will follow the devil's way. By using his divine power in the forceful exercise of political and military authority he can suppress disorder and justice in a moment. What quicker way could there be to fulfill God's purpose? The powers of the state can be used to forcefully straighten out the mess of human affairs. But that temptation too is rejected. The divine power is the power of servant love, and that alone can free men for their participation in God's purpose for their lives. This means, for example, that the church must resist the temptation to use the power of the state for its own institutional ends, and it means too that the church must help the state to limit the use of its power to its God-given purpose of maintaining order and justice.

Temptation 3: The devil takes Jesus to the Temple pinnacle, and tempts him to use his power in a direct religious display which will startle the world into the recognition that he is the Lord. Throw yourself down and let the crowds see the angels keep you from danger. But Jesus immediately refuses. There is no direct economic or political route to the Kingdom. Neither is there a direct religious or ecclesiastical way. There is only the way of servant love permeating all the institutions—economic, political, ecclesiastical. Then all these orders will play their God-given role in drawing the whole creation to a free participation in the way of Christ's love.

So Christ leaves the Messianic temptations behind. There are no shortcuts. He has been baptized into the humble role of the servant, and it is through that role that he calls the institutions to accept their God-given place in God's mission. So, too, the church must be trained to follow its Lord, taking that servant way into the institutions of the world so that they may serve their place in God's mission.

In the temptations, then, the positive role of the institutions is still affirmed, but there is a clear warning against the misuse of their powers. And that leads us to the other side of the New Testament picture.

2. The limits to the functions of the state are stressed—the negative teaching.

a. I Cor., ch. 6. Christians are counseled not to go to law, not because the state lawcourts are unholy, but because the Christian community should point forward to the time when the rule of law will be superseded by the way of reconciliation in love. In this way the church is asked to show the provisional character of the state by revealing the way of life that has now been introduced by Christ and that will finally make the present law-keeping function of the state unnecessary.

b. Acts 5:29; Rev., ch. 13. The first passage still accepted the positive role of the state; it simply suggested its temporal limits. But these passages give a more direct limitation of the authority of the state at the point where the government misuses its power. In the story in The Acts, government officials tell the apostles to stop preaching because they are disturbing the peace. Peter and the apostles answer, "We must obey God rather than men."

This one has been easy for the church to accept. Here the government is resisted when it encroaches on the church's exercise of its institutional calling—its witness to Christ. But the church has been far less inclined to intervene when the state transgresses on other human rights. Then it has been inclined to quote Rom., ch. 13, about the "powers that be" being ordained of God, with the explanation that the church is not entitled to intervene in the state's exercise of its secular authority. Since the medieval settlement, with its doctrine of the two established arms of God's one government—church and state —the Catholic and Protestant churches have normally followed that line. But in doing so they have failed to fulfill a major role of the church in relation to the other institutions in that they have failed to take seriously the negative teaching of the New Testament.

c. Rev., ch. 13, is the most powerful expression of this negative teaching. It reflects a point where the state is using its power to dehumanize—to repress human freedom. It has arrogated to itself an authority over men which belongs to God alone. It is demanding that men accept the authority of the state over their destiny and that they should swear unlimited obedience to the Emperor—

"Caesar is Lord." As a result the Seer now judges her to be "the beast out of the abyss." The church that knows that Christ is Lord is called to declare that the state has become demonic.

Behind this teaching is the belief of the time that the state was under an angelic power (*exousia*). This power has been created by God to serve him, but can rebel against him and claim a messianic role for itself. When that happens the church is called to expose those false messianic claims. By rejecting the false confession "Caesar is Lord," the church also calls the state back to its more humble, intended role. To say "Christ is Lord" means to identify with those who are oppressed by the rebellious state, and to suffer with them in resistance to the oppressor.

The particular "angelic-demonic" picture of the New Testament may need a little demythologization today. Not much, however. For surely we see here a realistic and contemporary task for the church in resisting the state's escalation of its role and powers to the point where power is used messianically. Then the task of witness is not limited to the verbal role of protest. The servant role Christ has pioneered requires active identification with the resistance in the attempt to bring the state back to its positive role of an orderly meeting of human needs. The church is called to resist the constant temptation of the powerful state to feed on its power, until at last it makes the demonic claim that it can solve the world's problems by the direct exercise of its political and military might.

The role of the church that is assumed in all this New Testament teaching has behind it the dominating vision of the final transformation of the world—"the new heaven and the new earth." The writers had no doubt that everything—every person, group, institution, even nature would be brought into the perfection of Christ's life (Eph. 1:9–10). They had no doubt that all the institutions—church, family, labor, government—had God-given roles in the movement to that goal. But they were sure that Christ had created the church as his primary instrument in carrying out his purpose. The community life of the church was to be the point where his purpose comes to visibility—the city set on the hill—and the place where men are trained in the way of Christ to be leaven that penetrates the other institutions with God's purpose.

This means, then, that Christians have to be aware of the place of these institutions in working toward that final goal. Certainly the church itself needs to become a demonstration community in which the world can see how the forces that bar the way to true community are overcome by the power of servant love. But a demonstration community exists precisely so that what is being demonstrated can then be accepted elsewhere. Thus, the church has its second task: training members to take this way of Christ into the other institutions of the world so that they can find their God-given ministries. Then the church and the other institutions alike can find in the servant ministry of Christ the clue to the world's destiny. They can discover that this weak way of servant love has been shown by the surprising Christ of the cross to carry the secret of God's power to save the world.

CHAPTER VI

The Ministry of the Church

What Jesus meant by ministry he makes all too clear!
Take his saying in Mark 10:45: "The Son of man came
not to be ministered unto, but to minister, and to give his
life a ransom for many." He interprets his ministry in
terms of Isaiah's image of the Suffering Servant. And in
case we think he is speaking only of his own ministry, take
the saying to the disciples that immediately precedes it:

You know that those who are supposed to rule over the Gentiles lord it over them, and their great men exercise authority
over them. But it shall not be so among you; but whoever
would be great among you must be your servant, and whoever would be first among you must be slave of all. (Mark
10:42–44.):

His disciples took it for granted that greatness implies
superior place and status, but Jesus makes it clear that
true greatness is not lordly power but skilled servanthood,
and that servanthood is the God-given key to the world's
true future. It is that ministry—the way of "the lackey,"
as Father John McKenzie translates it[1]—that is the secret
of God's Kingdom. And into that servant way all his disciples are called—everyone a minister, a lackey.

It is essential, then, that the discussion of the ministry

should start, not with the small class of ordained ministers, but the whole Christian community. It is the community of the servant way. The whole Christian community is called to be a "kingdom of priests" (I Peter 2:5 and 9). In the Old Testament, "priest" was a term limited to a class within the church, and their essential service was to the church. In the New Testament the term "priest" is applied to the whole body, and their essential service is to the world. Now with Christ the period of separate preparation was over, and ministry was turned out to its task of penetrating the life of the nations.

This ministry of the whole church is suggested in many of the images. The whole church is called to be "the light of the world," "the salt of the earth," "leaven." All are incorporated into "the body of Christ" and share in the task of carrying on the ministry he exercised in his body during his life on earth. Baptism into the life of the church is incorporation into Christ's baptismal way. In that act he accepted servant responsibility for the sins of the world, and by accepting Baptism the people of the church confess that they are disciples whose concern is not to be ministered unto but to share Christ's ministry to the world.

The ministry of the church, then, is an extension of the ministry of Christ. That has been described in the tradition of the church under the three offices—*munus triplex* —of prophet, priest, and king. It can be quickly seen that these three offices are closely related to the marks of the church in the Reformation tradition. The church is, they said, where the Word is truly preached (prophet), Sacraments duly administered (priest), and godly discipline maintained (king).

Here a crucial problem emerges. This classical Reformation definition describes these roles in relation to the in-

ternal life of the church. The consequent temptation was
to forget that the exercise of these ministries in the church
is intended as preparation for the exercise of these ministries in the world by the church as a whole.

As we have seen, this ministry of the community to the
world has two aspects. One essential side is that the life of
the church itself should be a testing ground on which the
world can see true human existence being practiced. The
other side is that the people of God are to be trained
for servant life within the secular structures so that the
world may be helped to find the way to its maturity in
Christ.[2]

Often a contrast is made between the ministry of *renewal* in the church, so that the internal life of the church
is deepened, and the ministry of *mission* to the world, in
which the church is turned out toward the needs of the
world. The point we are making is that the ministry of the
church includes both, and that these two aspects are inseparable. To be concerned for inward renewal and to
forget that this new life is given for the service of the
world is to destroy the servant character of ministry. But
to be concerned for servant mission in the world and to
separate this from the life of the renewed community is
to forget that this community life is meant to be both a
sign of the new life the world needs and the source of servant life for the world.

THE ORDAINED MINISTRY: APOSTOLIC SUCCESSION?

When we turn from the participation of the whole
church in the ministry of Christ to the particular ministries in the church, we reach a point of maximum ecumenical disagreement. It is generally accepted that the
New Testament itself gives us no clear picture of church

order in those first years, but that not too many years after the New Testament period a Catholic order had become general across the church. What conclusion should be drawn from these two facts?

One conclusion, as expressed by the French Reformed theologian Roger Mehl, is that no particular order is essential to the life of the church. Mehl points out that in the classical Protestant definitions of the church there are specific statements about "a *congregation* of faithful people, where the *word* is truly preached and the *sacraments* duly administered," but there is never any specific reference in these Reformation documents to a particular order of ministry. The Reformers, like the New Testament, accepted the necessity for *an* ordered ministry so that true preaching and due administration of the Sacraments could be preserved, but they were quite prepared for the particular form to vary with the changing institutional relation of the church to the world.

The fact that the Catholic order emerged quite quickly after the New Testament era simply means that it proved to be an effective order in the particular political and social situation of that time. Soon it was buttressed by arguments about bishops as inheritors of apostolic authority and as hierarchical channels for the continuing flow of Christ's grace within the church. But these arguments too are reflections of the contemporary attitudes toward order and authority. In the Reformation period the changing situation in northern Europe meant that the Catholic order as it had developed through the feudal period was no longer effective. The church was then free to reorder its internal ministry so that it could better serve its task of equipping the church for its ministry in the world of that time.[3]

A radically different interpretation of the same facts is given by contemporary "Catholics." Anglican Alan Richardson argues that the "apostolic" character of the ministry is understood only when we see that the church order which emerged by the time of Clement of Rome and Ignatius of Antioch—the familiar Catholic form— was the gift of the Spirit to the church to enable it to carry on its apostolic ministry in the postapostolic period.

The development of this apostolic ministry must be viewed in the same way as the development of the apostolic canon of Scripture and the apostolic Creed. Each of these was inspired by the Spirit so that the purity of witness given by the apostles in their lifetime could be carried on in the church after their death.

Richardson refuses to take a "fundamentalist" view of this Catholic order, however, just as he refuses to take a fundamentalist view of the Scriptures or the Creed. Each must be interpreted historically. With the order of the ministry we must ask: What was the historically intended shape of ministry that the Catholic order expressed? How would this historical intention express itself now in our situation? If those tests were to be applied, Richardson suggests, "None of the churches or denominations of the world Christian community today would find occasion for complacency or for pointing to the mote in their brother's eye."[4]

How can we decide between such opposed alternative explanations of the same facts? Not by an analysis of the particular New Testament texts that refer to the ministry. The disagreement is not on those but on the historical question of the way in which God directs the church in its mission in the world. Only by an exploration of that broader framework of the church's mission in the world in the light of the Christ event can we hope to resolve such a difference.

In this connection a case study of the different roads taken by two followers of Bultmann in their investigation of diversities of order in the New Testament is instructive. Hans Küng explores the roads followed by Ernst Käsemann and H. Schlier as they investigated this movement from diversity of order in the New Testament to the emergence in the pastoral epistles of the office of the bishop as the one in whom apostolic authority is centered and through whom the presence of the Spirit in the church is regulated.[5]

Käsemann sees this development as without authority for the continuing church. We are required to judge such developments from the center of the gospel, with its word of justifying grace. We then can see the trend to an authoritative order with a hierarchical center as "catholic decadence" in which the Pauline legacy recedes before the Judaic as the church developed a safer system of order. Apostolic legates (Titus, Timothy) were seen as standing in succession to the apostles in the same way as the rabbi stood in succession to Moses and Joshua.

Schlier sees this as a genuine apostolic provision for the continuity of the faith at the end of the apostolic period. We are not justified, he claims, in making such distinctions within the canon of Scripture and judging the final developments to be "catholic decadence." On the contrary, we must see this as a God-inspired means by which the continuity of apostolic substance is provided for from within the diversities of order reflected in the New Testament.[6]

The key question here is our historical understanding of the New Testament church. Both Käsemann and Schlier agree that there are diversities of order in the New Testament churches. Both agree that at the end the Catholic order was emerging. The question is: Does the final product become determinative? What then would be the meaning of the earlier diversity?

I would argue that the diversity represents the freedom of the church to order its ministries for effective witness within particular historical situations. The Jerusalem church order was different from the order of the Pauline churches in Asia Minor, for the reason that ministry was being related to quite different social settings. But that does not require us to say that the emergence of Catholic order represents a failure to stay within the freedom of the gospel. As the church began to move across the Roman Empire it faced the question of how the continuity of apostolic faith and life and the unity of the church could be maintained. It gave several related answers: a canon of Scripture with an authoritative account of the story, a summary of the central meaning of the faith in the Apostles' Creed, an apostolic ministry that had responsibility for the faith and for the unity of the church. This kind of order was suitable for the stage of history on which the church was entering as it moved out into the Roman world. If the church were now to be a demonstration community as a sign of God's purpose, the crumbling unity of the old Empire would soon need the emerging unity of the church to point the way to the future.

This does not mean that Käsemann's "catholic decadence" point is without foundation. Some of the exclusivistic and authoritarian claims that grew up with the emerging Catholic order illustrate only too well the constant tendency of the church to give itself the kind of security that will protect it from the need to face the changes that time inevitably brings. As a result the church made itself insufficiently free for new responses to the needs of mission in later periods, with a result that times of change too often became times of schism.

Here two factors are in tension. The original diversity in church order points to the freedom of the gospel— the flexibility given to the church to respond to different historical situations. The emerging Catholic tradition points to the need for keeping the apostolic substance of the faith and the apostolic unity of the community. Diversity of forms easily leads to loss of substance in the attempt to relate the church to different cultures, and to the splintering of the church. On the other hand, an authoritative order of continuity easily becomes inflexible, so that it is not free to relate to changing missionary situations.

If the postapostolic church faced the first danger, Luther faced the second. He had to appeal to the apostolic spirit and to the freedom of the gospel against the apostolic order in which the gospel had become imprisoned. He was able to do it by appealing behind the Catholic order to the original diversity of order in the New Testament. Luther knew the tension, however, and still prized the apostolic order if it could be renewed so that it could serve the gospel in the new situation.[7]

What is our situation today? How can we hold the truths in both sides of the tension in such a way as to discover the effective forms of ministry that are required today?

One proposal is included in the Australian scheme of union prepared by the Congregational, Methodist, and Presbyterian Churches. In asking what form of ministry is required now, the scheme suggests that it would not be enough for these three churches of the Reformed tradition to develop a ministry acceptable to themselves. The mission of the church in Australia requires that the church become a sign of a community that crosses the barriers of culture (white Australia in colored Asia), nation, race, caste, and class. In short, there is urgent need for the power of the church to transcend these divisions to appear—to become visible. As it was asked what form of ministry would best serve this need the answer was given: an apostolic ministry symbolizing the unity of the church across time and space, but reformed in such a way as to direct the ministry into the structures of contemporary need. For that reason the suggestion was that these Australian churches should reach out to the Church of South India and, through uniting their ministry with hers, symbolize the unity of the church across the most acute divisions of the world that are represented in Australia's relation to her neighbors. Suggestions were made also as to how the threefold order of Catholic tradition may be reformed to enable effective ministry in the contemporary scene.[8]

This tension on the level of church order has a deeper tension in the gospel that lies behind it. We have referred previously to the tension between the horizontal and vertical realities in the life of the church; we have pointed now to much the same tension between continuity in church order across space and time, with the need also for flexibility in relating order to particular situations. The roots of these tensions can be traced back to Christ's relation to the world. Leuba speaks of the way in which the titles given to Christ reflect a deep duality in his relation to the history of Israel.[9] On the one hand there are *institutional* titles which describe the essential continuity of his life and mission with the structures of Israel's history. He is called Son of David, King of Israel, Christ the Temple. On the other hand there are *spiritual* titles which emphasize the newness of his work as a vertical breaking into the continuity of Israel's life. He is called Son of Man, the New Creation, Servant, Lord. So his ministry expresses both continuity with the history of redemption and a freedom that leads to real tension with that history—a tension that can lead to a tragic break between the old Israel and the new community of Christ. The break is not the intention, and God's purpose is the restoration of continuity. But God's redeeming work involves new breakthroughs in relating his saving presence to the needs of the world, and if the continuing order resists, the tension may result in a break.

We have already rehearsed in brief form the way in which this tension is reflected in the New Testament picture of the apostles.[10] Now we must pursue this picture farther in search of a clue as to how the horizontal (Catholic) and vertical (Protestant) views may best be reconciled in the ministry of the church in our time.

Jesus did not choose the apostles at the beginning of his ministry. First he gathered the wider community of disciples, and then from their number chose the twelve whom he called apostles. This smaller group has a double function. It is responsible for leadership in the larger community of disciples, and it also has the responsibility for being the spearhead in the mission of the larger community in the world.

Here again we see reflected some of the characteristics of the church's ministry that have already occupied our attention. The ministry of the whole body of disciples comes first, and the representative ministry has two purposes: helping the community grow up into mature discipleship and leading them in their ministry to the world. We have noticed that in the letters of the New Testament, ministry out in the structures of the world receives little emphasis, but in the Gospels, movement out into the world receives a much greater stress.

These differences in emphasis, no doubt, reflect different situations of mission rather than different concepts of mission. The Gospels reflect the life of Jesus and his disciples in the familiar Jewish world where they had much greater freedom of access to the structures of need than did the early church when it first began its movement out into the world of the Gentiles. In both situations, however, the ministry of the leaders has the same twofold pattern: helping the community grow in maturity and leading the mission into the world.

We should not think of these apostles as democratically elected leaders of the disciples—Christ appointed them directly. A heated discussion has gone on among Biblical scholars as to the nature of this apostolic authority.[11] Some have argued that the apostles' relation to Christ is the same as that of a *shaliach* to a man of authority in the Old Testament (II Chron. 17:7–9). A man of authority could bestow his full personal authority on an ambassador so that "the one whom a man sends is the equivalent of himself."[12]

In support of that position a passage such as John 13:20 is quoted: "Truly, truly, I say to you, he who receives anyone whom I send receives me; and he who receives me receives him who sent me." (See also Matt. 10:40 and Luke 10:16.) Christ, the plenipotentiary or *shaliach* of the Father, sends the apostles in his name and as his plenipotentiaries. The Twelve also are given the role of the twelve patriarchs of Israel. "As my Father appointed a kingdom for me, so do I appoint for you that you may eat and drink at my table in my kingdom, and sit on thrones judging the twelve tribes of Israel." (Luke 22:29–30.) During the lifetime of Jesus, this argument continues, this sending forth with plenipotentiary authority was sporadic, as it was with the Jewish *shaliach*. But after Pentecost, the apostles became permanent plenipotentiaries on the mission from Jerusalem to Judea, to Samaria, and on to the ends of the earth (Acts 1:8).

What is at stake here? The argument is used by some Catholics (Anglo and Roman) to support the view that the apostles and their successors (bishops) were given plenipotentiary authority in the church, and that a hierarchical structure is inherent in its nature, with power flowing from Christ through his apostles (bishops) into the church as a whole.

We should immediately admit that the church is a community ruled "from above" by Christ. This has been recognized constantly by the church in its faith that Christ calls and equips those he appoints to particular ministries, so that the church's choice of ministers is not by democratic election but through the recognition of those whom Christ has elected. But this does not mean that the human authority system within the church is inherently hierarchical. Christ gives to Peter the power to forgive sins, but he gives the same authority to the whole body of disciples (John 20:19–23). So Peter speaks of the whole community as a kingdom of priests, while Paul speaks of the whole church as ambassadors carrying his plenipotentiary powers.

Even more important, the authority of Christ is the authority of servant love, and by its nature it is community-creating, not hierarchical. Those who have authority learn to use it as those who have it not, and the greatest is the one who is the servant of all. The world is to see in the Christian community a brotherhood in which the authoritarian patterns of the world's life have given way to the authority of servant love.

This does not mean that apostles do not exercise direct authority. They do. But it is the servant character of that leadership that accounts for the surprisingly free internal church structures that are reflected in the New Testament.

Several further features of the apostolic office need to be noted:

1. *There is an unrepeatable character about the office.*

They were the original foundation upon which the church was built—the Twelve who renewed the foundations of Israel for the final stage of God's mission. Among the Twelve, Peter was the foundation spokesman, the rock on whose confession the church was founded.

In this foundation function no one is needed to succeed to the office of the Twelve or of Peter. If Peter is first given the keys of the Kingdom after he is the first to confess that Jesus is the Christ (Matt. 16:17–19), this is followed (ch. 18:18) with the same gift to the whole community of disciples. "Truly, I say to you, whatever you bind on earth shall be bound in heaven, and whatever you loose on earth shall be loosed in heaven." Peter and the apostles are the first, but after the foundation is laid, ministry passes to the whole community.

2. *This apostolic foundation continues to be the basis for the church's life.*

The apostles did choose leaders for the churches they founded, so that a succession of ordered leadership was maintained. But when they ordained "in every church" "elders" to exercise leadership (Acts 14:23), they did not need to hand on their own office. The foundation work was complete, and that apostolic foundation is the continuing basis for the life of the church. Future leaders are responsible for keeping the church in continuity with the apostolic word, Sacraments, fellowship, and liturgy (ch. 2:42).

Care for this continuity is underlined by the apostolic practices:

a. For ordination they used the method of laying on of hands, just as in Judaism it was used for the ordination of rabbis. Like the rabbis the elders were to be responsible for the continuity of the faith.

b. In the Jerusalem church the *Sanhedrin* form of government was apparently followed, whereas in the Pauline churches the simpler *synagogue* pattern was the norm. In the former a high priest (James) presided over the chief priests and the elders, while in the latter the body of elders was presided over by one of their number. After the death of the apostles the former pattern became predominant and led to the threefold order of ministry that appears so prominently in the writings of Ignatius. But in both there is the same clear concern for continuity of leadership, with responsibility for being the bearers of the apostolic word, Sacraments, and fellowship within the community.

3. *The apostolic office calls for continuity, but it also calls for openness to the freedom of God's mission.*

In Luke's Gospel, the mission of the Twelve is paralleled by the mission of the Seventy. The terms of their mission are the same, for they represent Christ in the same way (see Luke 10:1–6). In Christian tradition this symbolism is taken to mean that Christ's mission first is to Israel (the twelve tribes) but that it is now ready also for all the nations (the seventy). The apostolic ministry breaks out of its limits to reach out universally. But, as we know, this newness stretched the continuity with Israel to the breaking point.

In Chapter III we referred to the rough edges around

H

the neat picture of the twelve apostles as indicating this stretching toward the new. Paul's new task goes beyond that which can be borne by the symbol of the Twelve. He is born out of due time—a specially created apostle to the Gentiles. James, Christ's brother in the flesh, is also an extra and seems to represent in contrast, as the Davidic-line leader of the Jerusalem church, a solid form of institutional continuity. Paul's is the vertical apostleship, James's the horizontal one. The tension between them was always close to the breaking point, with Peter feeling each pull so strongly that he vacillated before finally acceding to Paul's insistence that unity in the Christian community has priority over the continuity of Jewish cultic practices (Gal. 2:11 ff.). According to the story in the Acts (ch. 10:9 ff., the vision of the unclean creatures) it took a divine intervention before Peter was free enough to accept this new stage of God's mission. It took a council of the whole church (Acts, ch. 15) before others were willing to move in the new direction.

In this tension we see again the duality of the institutional and the spiritual, the horizontal and the vertical, and we see this tension close to the breaking point. But this aspect of the picture of the apostolate does give us a pointer toward the way in which we can relate the conflicting views of those who see the emerging Catholic order as the norm for the church and those who see the fracturing of that order in the Reformation as a reassertion of the freedom of the church's order for new situations of faithfulness.

On one side of this tension in the apostolic office we have James, a reminder that there is an unbroken continuity in the redemption story and that there are apostolic foundations with which the church must preserve continuity.

Here we can see why the church can value the symbol of episcopal order stretching back across the centuries to the postapostolic period and linking the church across the divided cultures of the earth. This continuity and symbol of unity can be valued as God's good gift which the Catholic world has kept in treasure for the whole church.

On the other side we have Paul, a warning against believing that institutional continuity is a guarantee of faithfulness to Christ. Paul had to stand against Peter and James. The line of continuity had to be broken open for the new obedience that was now required. At the time of the Reformation the tension again reached the breaking point—and this time the line of continuity was insufficiently flexible to contain the new form of obedience.

In any effective church union scheme, then, both realities should be taken into account. Catholic order can be willingly accepted as a symbol of restored continuity, so long as this recognition does not cast doubt upon the genuineness of the obedience involved in the Reformation ministries. It was this double truth that the Church of South India sought to express. They accepted both Catholic and Reformation orders at the time of union, while providing for the future restoration of the unity of these ministries under the Catholic order. Many believe that rather than allowing for a period of growing together as in South India, it is better to find a way of integrating the ministries from the beginning. If that can be done in such a way that both the horizontal and vertical realities are affirmed by a clear witness,[13] and if it is made clear that acceptance of Catholic order does not bring with it authoritarian hierarchical views of the church, then all right. What is vital is that the true nature of authority in the church's life under the authority of Christ be made clear, and that the necessary freedom of the church for new forms of obedience to Christ's mission in the world be affirmed.

THE ORDAINED MINISTRY: OFFICE AND FUNCTION

The New Testament recognizes that if the many gifts distributed among the members are to be used for the common good, a ministry of oversight is required. A distinction is required, however, between the ministerial *office* and the ministerial *functions*. In passages such as Acts 14:23 and in various texts in Timothy, the appointment of elders is to an office of oversight. But in the passage in Eph., ch. 4, where it speaks of "some . . . apostles, some prophets, some evangelists, some pastors and teachers," the reference is to ministerial functions. There is no fixed relation between the office and the functions. Rather, the office has the responsibility for seeing that the varied gifts of ministry within the church are ordered for the common good.

Unfortunately, those in office often forget that it exists only to serve the community. Forgetting the warning of Christ against seeing their office as a superior status (Mark 9:34–35), they think in terms of "pre-eminence" rather than service (III John 9).

The result of this is the periodic revolt against "clericalism," and a periodic attempt to abolish separate ordained ministries in the hope that the laity as a whole will assume the responsibilities of ministry. But the experience of the centuries is that abolition of clerics is no cure of clericalism. Soon leaders emerge again from the community who assume the same traditional roles:

—responsibility for preaching and teaching—the prophetic office;

—responsibility for Sacramental and liturgical life—the priestly office;

—responsibility for pastoral care and rule—the pastoral office.

Such a ministry is required to carry responsibility for the apostolic faith and to order the training of the laity for their ministry. The threefold office of Christ's ministry is refracted through the threefold office of the ordained ministry into the life of the laity as they are trained to exercise this office in the world.

The ordained ministry exercise the threefold office in a representative way in the church so that the laity can exercise this ministry of Christ in a representative way in the world. Because that is the role of the ordained, "ministerial training" has historically been seen as training men for the prophetic, priestly, and pastoral roles. Today, however, this training process is in severe difficulties from two sides:

1. The actual operation of the ordained ministry today no longer seems to reflect this threefold office in any satisfactory way. A World Council of Churches "Study on Patterns of Ministry and Theological Education"[14] refers to studies in various countries which arrive at the same general picture.[15] Today the minister is spending far more time in the tasks of administrator and organizer than in the traditional roles of prophet, priest, and pastor. In consequence, ministers have a strong sense of frustration in the feeling that their real office is not adequately reflected in the roles they are performing. These "contemporary" roles of administrator and organizer, which consume so much of their time, are not integrated into their theological self-understanding. The result is that the ministry is facing a major identity crisis. This is intensified

by the fact that even the traditional functions are being redefined in a nontraditional direction. The pastoral role, for example, has been radically redefined under the influence of clinical psychology, with the result that it too is no longer effectively related to the received theological understanding of the office.

2. If the actual operation of the ministry no longer adequately reflects the threefold office, so also the structures of the church no longer effectively relate the ministry of the laity to the structures of human existence in today's world. As the World Council of Churches study on the Missionary Structure of the Congregation has revealed so clearly, the radical changes in the institutional life of the world occasioned by the urban-technological developments of our time now call for radical changes in the way Christian ministry is related to our world. Those changes are now occurring but in this period of transition there is again a strong identity crisis in the church as the task of relating structures of ministry to structures of need is being carried through.

What can be done? Part of the answer to the problem of the self-image of ministers would seem to lie in the redefinition of the received theological image of the ministry to relate it to the secular age in which this ministry must now be exercised. The problem is not that the three offices are now out of date but that the way these have been defined is now out of date. We have to lift the ministerial image out of the simpler context of the rural society in which it has always been carried on, and reset it in the more complicated structures of the urban-technological society.

In rural community life there were always tasks of organization and administration. But because they came in the context of immediate personal relations the tasks were seen as pastoral. In the impersonal structures of our life, however, the inevitably much greater organizational and administrative tasks are not easily integrated into the image of "pastor"! But this does not mean that these tasks are foreign to the ministerial office. On the contrary. Since increased organizational and administrative responsibilities are a feature of the institutional life of our urbanized society, it is urgent that some way be found of relating Christian ministry to this new mode of human existence. If the "pastoral" image of the office as Christ as the servant King is not able adequately to express this role, then a new image will be required.

The Working Group in East Germany for "The Missionary Structure of the Congregation" study included this statement in its report.

It seems to us that perhaps the greatest hindrance in the way of a missionary church today is the self-understanding of the pastor and the congregation. . . . The idea has wormed its way into the mind of the pastor and the congregation, of the pastor as the one who always gives and the congregation as those who only receive. . . . This image does not include the concept that members of the flock give shepherd service to one another (*prosechein*: Acts 20:28, cf. Luke 17:3; *episkopein*: Acts 20:28, cf. Heb. 12:15; *parakelein*: I Tim. 4:13, Titus 2:15, cf. I Thess. 5:11, Heb. 3:13; *didaskein*: I Tim. 6:2, cf. Col. 3:16); And that they are sent into a hostile world (Matt. 10:16). . . .

This picture hinders the understanding of the congregation as a sent troop, and thus of its apostolic "go-structure," and it has created the structure of the one-man system of pastoral care, and the corresponding "come-structure" to which pastor and congregation are accustomed.[16]

I would add that the pastor image is unsuitable also to the task of relating the servant work of Christ to the highly structured forms of urban life. The need is to integrate into the self-image of the ministry a positive understanding of the organizational and administrative tasks.

That brings us, however, to the second problem. Ministers feel guilty about the time spent on organization and administration, not just because these roles have not been integrated into their self-image, but because they feel that they spend their time organizing and administering a largely irrelevant structure. After expending all that time and energy they are not able to see the ministry of the church being channeled into the structures of the world. Instead, the church is largely isolated from the places where ministry is urgently required.

We will return to this need to re-form the structures of the church.[17] Here we can simply notice that already major changes are taking place. All across the church we are witnessing experiments with new forms of ministry. Many attempts are being made to penetrate the public worlds, such as industry, politics, education, leisure. Efforts are also being made to renew the local congregation in the residence community so that it can minister effectively to its private world.

These developments give rise to the question of how the two forms of ministry—"inner-directed" to enable the church to display in its own life the new community existence in Christ, and "outer-directed" to lead the church to its service within the secular structures—can be effectively related to each other. One attempt to answer this has been made by a theologian from Taiwan, C. H. Hwang.[18] He suggests that we should think in terms of a threefold focus of ministry: "God-directed," "church-directed," and "world-directed." The first, however, scarcely seems to belong in a separate category, for all Christian ministry needs to be God-directed in the double sense of being under God's direction and directed to God. Hwang, in fact, turns most of his attention to the other two. He then suggests that in today's world the world-directed ministries will be taking more manpower and more resources than the church-directed ministries. With the rapid changes in the secular world and the great needs for ministry within those changes this is inevitable and proper. Ministry within the church as a separate community will still be needed, but the focus of major attention will be on "the church for the world."

VARIETIES OF MINISTRY

That we are now witnessing the passing of the dominance of the single form of ministry that marked the centuries of rural existence seems clear.[19] The village congregation with its local pastor had a great history. The church at the center of the village was able to serve as a powerful symbolic expression of Christ as Lord. The minister at the center of the congregation was also in a position to help the laity relate their lives to the available range of secular concerns, and usually that range was sufficiently limited for one man to be able to lead the congregation in relating their faith to those concerns. That they all too often failed to do so is obvious; that the structure was one that made it possible is the point.

This single form came to a brilliant late flowering in early New England. The parson at the center of those village communities became very often the model that the laity followed in the task of wresting their new human existence from the unwilling wilderness. He was the model household head, the model farmer, the schoolteacher. These roles had a greater authority because he was also the sacral center of village life by virtue of being the God-appointed pastor of the church. It was generally believed that it was only as the supernatural forces of the divine life subdued the unruly forces of men and of nature that a community could be established in which the life of the city of God would be reflected and in which the task of subduing the earth could be carried on. These supernatural forces were available only through faithful worship in the holy community. Our latter-day assumption that the divine forces of order are available to us through scientific discovery and that the servant ministries of the church can be exercised through the struggle to direct these powers to the human good was to them completely foreign. The struggle to order the unruly powers of nature began in the sacral life of the church. The central place of the parson in that sacral life reinforced his role as the model of the way the divine order could then penetrate life's daily affairs.

The incredible number of clergy and sons of clergy populating the pages of early American history gives eloquent witness to the power of the model of ministry they provided. But the passing power of that model can equally be seen in the passing of that clerical domination in the pages of *Who's Who*. In our communities there is now no single sacral center. Varieties of "priests" are now represented in the various worlds of our culture. Whereas they lived in the world of the "first nature" and felt that the power to order the unruly forces of that nature came directly from God through the sacral life of the church, we live in the world of the "second nature" in which the power to control the forces of nature is within the hands of the priests of science and technology. Direct appeal to God has now become indirect. Here again we can see the need for the ministries of the church to be diversified for effective relation to these centers of human and scientific order. Now no single model of ministry can serve to symbolize the Lordship of Christ over life. As ministry diversifies with the diversification of the centers of life, so also ministry is declericalized with the increasing secularization of life. Now the ministries of the laity within these secular structures have become correspondingly important.

There are then two reasons for the decline of the power of the single form of ministry. One is the passing of the village with its single center and the rise of the multiple-centered world of urban society. The other is the death of the sacral view of society in which the priest served as the symbolic point of entrance for divine order into the unruly world of nature.

How is the church responding to these changes?

One inevitable reaction is a strong conservative attempt to refurbish the model. In the United States this attempt has been given great strength by the power of a religious nostalgia which has become deeply intertwined with a strong conservative resistance to many of the changes that are accompanying the rise of the urban-technological society. The conservative climate of resistance to such social change has given a considerable "success" to the village type of congregation, particularly in the white culture of the South and in the suburbs of the North. But the price has been that these congregations have not been able to relate the faith to the phenomena of urban life. The priest is no longer the sacral center through whom the divine order can flow into the structures of life. He is no longer the model through whom a style of life is fashioned so that the congregation can see the way to relate the life of faith to the life of the world. Too often, instead, he is the priest of the passing order—symbolically blessing the nostalgic resistance to the changes that threaten the congregation's privileged ways.

This is not to say that congregations in residence communities can no longer be places for relevant ministry. But it is to say that they can no longer continue that ministry in the same way. Because the structures of life have altered, the structures of ministry must be reshaped. The Lordship of Christ will less and less be witnessed to from a single center above society, or above the congregation. The raised pulpit in the church at the village center, with the spire pointing to the heavens and the high altar drawing us to the sacred point at which divine order enters into daily life—this is less and less the way in which faith is felt and in which ministry is exercised. Now we hear of Christ coming to man as the servant who is present at the places where the decisions are being made which determine the future. And with this we are moving away from the cleric as the sacred figure lifted up above the daily rhythms and symbolizing the point of Christ's entrance into life. Instead, we are moving into a time of variety of ministries, whose characteristic will be immersion in the diverse structures of contemporary life and whose function will be to evoke the health-giving form of Christ at the places where the shape of human life is being determined.

Will this mean that "worker-priests" will now become the norm? Will it mean that the distinction between "ordained" and "lay" will no longer be clear, with the emphasis being upon the calling of the whole community of the church to ministry in the world? The precise answers to such questions are not yet known. One thing seems evident: Ordained ministers will no longer be sacral figures in the sense we have been describing. But this does not mean that the church has less need of ordained men. Because the Christian faith centers in a story there will still be the same roles of "guarding the tradition," and of leading the community in the discovery of how to participate in God's ongoing story.

Christ chose leaders whom he made responsible for the story, and for training the community in the way of discipleship. The *form* of that leadership has changed considerably down through the centuries as the forms of society and of man's view of the world have altered. But the *tasks* of that leadership have continued and are no less needed today. The continuity of the ministry is in the unbroken need to guard the story and to train the people of God for participation in Christ's mission.

OVERSIGHT IN THE CHURCH

"God has appointed in the church," says Paul, certain people to certain duties (I Cor. 12:28; cf. Rom. 12:3–8). There was no one uniform style of leadership in the New Testament churches, but there was a real continuity of functions, offices, and order in the midst of the variety.

The continuity of *functions* we have described in terms of continuing responsibility for telling the story (guarding the tradition) and for training the membership for discipleship with Christ and participation in his mission.

The continuity of *offices* we have traced to continuing participation in the threefold office of Christ as prophet, priest, and king.

The continuity of *order* is less obvious. The widespread acceptance of the Catholic episcopal order as a symbolic expression of the continuity of apostolic authority in an ordered ministry of oversight has come into conflict with the views that *episcopē* ("oversight") draws its authority only from continuing witness to apostolic truth. The ancient horizontal order is no automatic guarantee of the continuity of apostolic life, and God has on occasion broken through that order with vertical witnesses to the truth. Nevertheless, we are justified in valuing the horizontal symbol of continuity of order and in working to reunite the horizontal and vertical witnesses to the church's continuing apostolic mission.

Having said this much we must face a profound question that hangs over all this traditional emphasis on the continuity of the ministry. Does all the talk of unchanging "divine offices" depend for its authentication on a metaphysical view that is now disintegrating? Does the death of the sacral attitude mean that all offices are laicized, in the sense that leadership is simply a function of the human situation which must be ordered according to pragmatic tests of effectiveness?

To be more specific: Were not the preaching, sacramental, and pastoral offices so filled with sacral assumptions that they were divine channels of grace, that they now must be radically redefined if they are to express leadership of the people of God in the servant ministry of Christ within the secular world of our time?

There is no doubt that the inherited forms did become filled with the content of a now vanishing metaphysical world view. There is a need to free them from that context, and to redefine the offices and order within our world view. The offices will continue, but the way the story is told, the manner in which the community's participation in that story is celebrated, and the form of pastoral responsibility in the community and for servant responsibility beyond it will be subject to considerable change.

Similarly, while episcopal order will probably be even

more widely accepted in the church, a more varied expression of this task of oversight seems to be required. There have been, for example, suggestions for a "group episcopacy," with a team of bishops carrying joint responsibility for coordinating the increasing varieties of ministry needed for today's world. One bishop may have oversight of ministers to the world of the family; another of ministers to business, industry, and politics; another of ministers to arts, education, leisure, etc., with the team carrying group responsibility for planning and coordinating the mission in a region.

It must be said further that this rethinking of the way in which the offices and order will be continued in our time also involves a radical rethinking of the relation between the ordained and the lay ministries. Ours is now a multi-centered world, and the different worlds call for different applications of the story, different forms of gathering for training, and different styles of service. As specialized ministries are now becoming more and more varied, the lines that distinguished clergy and laity in the past are becoming less and less clear. The leader in one world may do little in the way of formal preaching or little in the way of formal administration of the Sacraments, but he may have heavy responsibility for theological judgment as he seeks to lead the people in their servant task in that particular world.

Who should be ordained? Only those with responsibility for leadership in the three offices within a congregation? Or those with major leadership responsibilities of quite varied types? And who shall decide which leadership responsibilities call for ordination as over against those which can properly be carried on by laymen?

In the classical Protestant tradition a great deal of emphasis has been placed on the New Testament teaching

of "the priesthood of all believers," with it still being affirmed that a ministry of oversight is needed to train the
laity for their universal priesthood. The distinction between the two levels of ministry was related to a distinction between the two realms: the church, where the Word
is preached, Sacraments administered, and pastoral care
given, and the world where the secular ministries are carried on. In the sacred sphere of the church, the ordained
ministry are given leadership, and in the secular sphere
of the world, the laity have the responsibility.

This separation between the two spheres has now well-
nigh collapsed. The ministries of oversight are now increasingly being dispersed into the secular worlds, and leadership is more and more seen as the task of leading the
way in the discovery of the servant life within the structures of the society. The church is not so much a separate
sphere—the sacred in contrast to the secular—as the piece
of the world that is conscious of Christ's purpose for it.
As such the church can be dispersed within the various
structures of society with varied forms of leadership, reflecting the varied forms of its presence and service.

The problem we are discussing is well illustrated in
Karl Rahner's book *Theology for Renewal*.[20] In that book
Rahner gives a rather traditional statement of the given
office and function of "the priest." He is, first and foremost,
the one who stands before the altar and in his Sacramental
role figures forth the truth that Christ is the consecrator
of the whole creation. This objective and inner-churchly
role is his first task. But there is a second outward-worldly
role to his priesthood that is inseparable from it. In this
second role it becomes clear that the objective truth of
Christ as the consecrator is a living truth that happens
in the world. Precisely because his first role is that of a
priest making present the mysteries of Christ, it is ines-

capable that the priest must also be "an apostle, an envoy, a witness, a teacher, a shepherd; one who comes down from the altar and goes out into the world to proclaim the message, to work and fight, in season and out of season, for the Kingdom of God; one who strives to subdue this earth to the reign of God."[21]

"If the priest as cult-man . . . withdraws to the altar . . . what he has done is to cease to be a cult-man of Christ. . . . Even more: . . . New Testament usage never designates the priest's office in terms of the language of cult but always that of apostolic and pastoral work. . . . A priest, then, is both a sacrificing priest and a pastoral priest in an interior, radical unity which involves both tasks in such fashion that neither can be truly fulfilled except in a mutual interpenetration."[22]

Here we see the problem. If the priest must follow his liturgical action "out into the world," following the Word as it subdues the earth to the reign of God, his very priesthood involves him in appropriate forms of presence in the worlds of contemporary life where the battles are being fought, where the key decisions are being made, and where the shapes of need are being formed. That cannot all be done from the traditional altar at the center of the residence community. That is why the worker-priests arose. They sought to follow the liturgical action into the alienated worlds where the hierarchical metaphysical form of priestly authority no longer exercised its power. It was an attempt to bring together again the two inseparable sides of priesthood. For this same reason we are witnessing a variety of experiments with forms of clerical presence in the secular structures.

A real question hangs over the cult with its altar. Does the altar have the kind of objective visibility today which Rahner assigns to it? Does it have a given place to stand outside history, as it were, as a sign of the consecration of the cosmos? Or is the altar itself found only on the movable stage of history and subject therefore to the changing forms of the historical process? This question revolves in Rahner's work around his treatment of "religion."

"Religion," he says, has two basic meanings for the Christian church:

1. It refers to the institutional bodily element of the faith—the given cultic forms with which Christ provided his church.

2. It refers also to the ethos of a particular period of history. The whole of the premodern age, and in particular the period of Christendom, was "religious." A mysterious religious world is assumed to surround our earthly existence, and it is to this religious world that the church has access.

In this second sense, Rahner says, religion is a thing of the past. Science has opened this world of mystery to men's exploration, and men are losing the sense of the cultic reality of the church as the access point to the religious world that surrounds the first nature. The technical, planned world of the second nature in which secular man lives calls for secular ministries to be fostered by the church in which the laity find the meaning of Christ for the world through a new this-worldly asceticism. This asceticism is one in which man is trained for true self-control "in regard to all those possibilities for self-indulgence and addiction which have now grown beyond all measurability."[23] This self-control which will free the disciplined man for the historical task God has for the secular world is "natural"; that is, it has to be worked out within secular life. But it is also "supernatural," in that without the grace of Christ it cannot be achieved.

So far Rahner is close to Bonhoeffer in the thesis that "religion" is dead. But he makes a distinction which Bonhoeffer (and Barth) did not. There is still a necessary religion in the sense of a cultic, institutional, given embodiment of the faith—a "sacred order" of "commandment, formula, law, authority, and order" which survives the passing of the religious ethos.

What is involved here? Bonhoeffer would agree that there is a givenness to the Christian faith, requiring an "arcane discipline" of prayer and fellowship that centers around the Bible and the Sacraments. But the difference would seem to be that for Bonhoeffer these can no longer be given a place beyond the changes of history. The classical metaphysical age spoke of a timeless order of ministry, celebrating a timeless liturgy in symbolically timeless language and music. The priests drew the people into their timeless world by presiding at the confessional with timeless doctrinal and moral authority. But that is no more. Just as Christ came to man as fully present in the temporal world, so all these functions must be seen as fully within history. The altar is no longer fixed. It is the altar of the living Christ, and celebration takes place around his moving presence.

It is inevitable that the church must attempt to give the living, moving mission of Christ in history some visible form around which we can gather and from which we can move. Such visibility of form in liturgy, in doctrine, and in order is essential for our existence in the flesh. But these religious forms are like law. Essential, they must also be seen as subject to constant change so that we may be free to move along with Christ in history with the changing shapes of obedience that his mission requires.

Similarly, the ministry in this flexible, multiple-formed

age does not require one fixed form. There will be a variety of ministries as servants of Christ gather the laity for their secular ministries. Ministries of oversight are required to relate the given story of the faith to the new situations where the story is being continued, and to pioneer in these new situations of ministry as an essential part of the task of training the laity for their service in unfamiliar places.

It can be said, then, that the basic character of ministry has not changed. Ministry is still drawn from Christ and is still exercised by the whole body under the leadership of those who are called by Christ to direct the community in its service. But the forms of this ministry are in the process of radical change. To make sense of those changes is both a theological and a sociological task—theological because it centers on Christ's moving presence, sociological because we must discern this presence within the structures of our society.

CHAPTER VII

The Secular Mission of the Church:
Service in the Structures of the World

The New Testament description of institutional life
within the orders of family, labor, government (we noticed
in Chapter V) no longer describes the institutional life
of our world. The rise of the urban society has been accompanied by the spinning away of major areas of human
existence from their former integrated place in the community of residence. These public worlds, such as politics,
industry, commerce, communications, education, enter-
tainment, leisure, are now separated from the private
world of the family. The result is that the church, whose
primary identification has been with the world of residence, is now developing an increasing variety of forms of
presence in these public worlds.

The first reaction might be to suggest that we need to
revise the simple New Testament system of orders which
reflected the rural world to take account of the more varied
system of orders that now marks our urbanized existence.
But this will not do. Not only does the continual process
of change mean that there is no stable configuration of
orders; the subtle interactions between them often mean
that the places of decision are not in the worlds themselves

but at shifting points of intersection. For example, problems such as poverty and race prejudice and war call for ministries that seek to penetrate the structures of decision at places that transcend the particular public worlds. Strategies are required at metropolitan, regional, national, and international levels. And for this reason we are seeing the emergence of new forms of ministry not only within the particular public worlds—such as industry—but in relation to broader configurations of life. For example, Metropolitan Associates of Philadelphia (MAP) is attempting to discover the broader shapes of decision-making in the metropolis and to plan its ministry at this more complex level.[1]

This complex and dynamic structure of the worlds that mark our life precludes us from beginning with a description of the orders and then proceeding to discuss how the church's mission can be carried out within them. Instead, I propose a different approach, beginning with a discussion of the forms of the church's witness within these structures under the time-honored rubric of "word" and "deed."

THE MINISTRY OF THE WORD WITHIN THE STRUCTURES: THE CHURCH AS "THE MOUTH OF GOD"

The churches have developed the habit in recent decades of making pronouncements on the major areas of institutional responsibility. Big questions arise in this connection. To whom are they addressed? To Christians, to guide them in their actions in the institutions? To non-Christians as well, so that the institutions as a whole can be called to their God-given responsibility? On what basis should they speak? On the explicit basis of the Christian faith? If so, do we expect non-Christians to understand them, or can they be expressed in common ethical language so that they can become the basis for common action extending beyond the community of confessing Christians?

The New Testament ethical sections in the epistles did relate "the Way" to the ethical struggles and language of the non-Christian world, so that Christians apparently had some basis for common action with non-Christians in these institutions. Nevertheless, these ethical attitudes were so deeply penetrated by their Christian faith that the call to Christians to act in a distinctive way seems to be dominant.

How should the church pursue this task now? In ecumenical documents there is a marked attempt to appeal to common moral principles recognized by Christians and non-Christians alike: justice, freedom, equality, human rights. But there is also the tendency to draw upon the distinctively Christian understanding of God's purpose and the relation between these two aspects is fitful and often confused.[2]

One reason for this is that the typical words in our common ethical vocabulary have no commonly accepted meaning today. In our varied ideological camps we speak of justice, peace, freedom, human rights, but we do not give them the same content or relate them in the same way to action. For this reason some have suggested that we should abandon all such attempts at common vocabulary ethics. All forms of "natural law" approach must be replaced by revealed ethics in which the direct demands of the way of God revealed in Christ become the form of our witness to the world.

If we did that, would this mean that non-Christians must first accept our faith before we could join with them in common action? Is there no common ground on which we can stand? We are faced here, I believe, with a false alternative. People of different faiths and ideologies use common words such as "justice," "freedom," "peace," because the common structures of human existence confront us with common human questions. These questions are our meeting ground, and it is vital that as Christians we meet with our fellow human beings on that ground.

What is also vital, however, is that we understand the nature of the meeting. The common words point to common questions, but they do not carry a common meaning. The meeting includes, therefore, a struggle to fill the words with meaning. Our witness means that we are seeking to fill them with the content given them by Christ. But how?

One answer is that we can do this effectively only as we are participants with our fellowman in the common human struggles, and that the content is offered not only in the witness of our words but in the form of our service.

Take an illustration. Perhaps the most powerful statement on a social issue that the World Council of Churches has made is the statement on race made by the Evanston Assembly in 1954. One reason is that here the churches were not speaking simply on the basis of abstract principles. The church was grappling with an urgent question for itself, and in the statement that emerged the words that are familiar to all were filled with content from the church's struggle concerning its own life in the light of the gospel.

The participants in the discussion at Evanston came from the midst of deep race tensions from all parts of the world, and they had to confront the fact that the powerful forces of race prejudice had bitten deeply into the life of the church itself. But there, in the context of an interracial, international assembly, they were deeply aware of the call of Christ for his community to reveal to the world a fellowship in which these prejudices are transcended by the power of his Spirit. They were conscious of the story of Pentecost, where the church was launched into the world as a community in which the barriers of race, language, caste, and class were overcome by the creative power of Christ's love. They knew that the church is called to be out in front of the strife-ridden communities of the world, showing them that there is a way through prejudice and fear to a community of equality, justice, and human rights for all.

The church, then, heard a word first to itself. In the context of the common questions of the world it heard the word of Christ spoken to it and through it to the world. But because the church spoke so strongly to its own community of the way of "justice" and "freedom" in Christ, its appeal could be heard far beyond the boundaries of the church. The common value words were given content because they were spoken from the life of the church and in the context of its witness to Christ's purpose to reconcile all things through the power of his servant love.

We must not stop there. The church's word requires the disciples to follow it into the places where the word becomes flesh. The witness of word from the church requires the witness of deed in the institutional life of the world. But here the record of our churches is very weak. If this requires that the church must witness (*a*) through showing the new way in its own life, as a community where the future is being revealed, and (*b*) through the way Christians are prepared to enter as servants into Christ's struggle in the world, we must admit that on both counts the church has been found wanting. There are, of course, notable exceptions—the remnant that has not bowed the knee to Baal—so that the content to which the words point has been given some visibility. But the record across the world on this major human issue of our time is one that would suggest that the church stands subject to the fires of God's institutional judgment.

A further important point arises. As the minority have moved out into the midst of this struggle for racial justice they have discovered themselves fighting beside those who make no Christian profession but who demonstrate the spirit of servant love. The Christians involved have recognized Christ at work beyond the boundaries of his visible church. There, in some sense, the real event of Christian life and obedience has occurred. For that reason so many theologians are speaking of the "latent church" beyond the boundaries of the "patent church," or the hidden community of Christ outside the visible community of those who confess him. It reminds us (as does the parable of the Last Judgment in Matt., ch. 25) that Christ can and does bypass the visible boundaries of his confessing community in his work in the world, gathering to himself a community of faithfulness around the places of human need.

An illustration of this is given by Bonhoeffer from his experience in the fight for values against the Nazis. He writes:

The deification of the irrational, of blood and instinct, of the beast of prey in man could be countered with the appeal to reason; arbitrary action could be countered with the written law; barbarity with the appeal to culture and humanity; the violent maltreatment of persons with the appeal to freedom, tolerance and the rights of man; the subordination of science, art and the rest to political purposes with the appeal to the autonomy of the various different fields of human activity.[3]

Then, in a passage that vividly illustrates how the common value words can become the meeting place where Christians and non-Christians can be drawn together by God in an alliance based upon a content in which the Christian recognizes the truth, Bonhoeffer continues:

It was clear that it was not the Church that was seeking the protection and the alliance of these concepts; but, on the contrary, it was the concepts that had somehow become homeless and now sought refuge in the Christian sphere, in the shadow of the Christian Church. . . . There took place a return to the origin. The children of the Church, who had become independent and gone their own ways, now in the hour of danger returned to their mother.[4]

This experience that Christian values can take on powerful life outside the boundaries of the church, and that in times of crisis they may seek a restored alliance with the family of their origin has been repeated over and again in the race crisis. Sometimes, all too rarely, this has given rise to effective coalitions, in which the true service of Christ has been carried on. Sometimes at the moment of coalition, it becomes apparent that these values in the course of their history outside the church have lost some of their essential content. Christians must then struggle to refill the words with true meaning and to keep the coalition faithful to Christ's purpose. But sometimes, on the other hand, unbelievers reveal a faithfulness to the true values which puts the believers to shame.

Such common concepts as justice, tolerance, freedom, equality, human rights, are the common arena on which Christians seek to come together with non-Christians in the secular ministry to which Christ calls them. The dialogue and common action that occur on this arena, however, call for considerable sophistication, for the same words can carry quite different content for different participants—as attempts to work with Communists have so often revealed. Here is a genuine struggle where we seek to work for the victory of Christ in bringing these words under obedience to his purposes. The awareness of this difficulty must not lead to withdrawal from the place of meeting. On the contrary, it is on this common meeting ground that the real struggle for meeting human need takes place, and it is in the battle as to which meaning shall give content to the common words that the battle for the emerging future is fought.

THE MINISTRY OF DEED WITHIN THE STRUCTURES: THE CHURCH AS THE SERVANT OF SECULAR INSTITUTIONS

As we have spoken of the church's role of verbal witness, we have emphasized the need for that word to issue in deed. What is being discovered is the need for the church to follow the word into the institutions of the world so that the laity can be trained for their service in the secular structures at the places where the real struggles are occurring. This is the reason for the "secular institutes," for the urban training centers which seek to train clergy to work with the laity in the midst of urgent metropolitan issues, for industrial missions, for vocational groups, for task forces on particular social and political problems. The church is not being faithful if it expects the laity as individuals to find the way of obedience in the complicated structures and situations of contemporary life. Instead, it is called to follow the word to the key places of obedience and there gather the laity for the understanding of the word where it must become flesh, and where that deed requires corporate form if the action is to be effective.

We can express the meaning of this church action in the world by drawing on three of the metaphors used by

Christ in his description of the life to which the church is called.

1. *The church is to be a city on a hill, a light shining into the darkness, a candle on a candlestick.* (Matt. 5:14–16.)

When Jesus called his disciples to let their light shine before men he was summoning the church to witness to him, not just through the words that directed the world's attention to him, but by a life that showed to the world the working out of God's purpose. "Let your light so shine before men, that they may see your good works and give glory to your Father who is in heaven." (Matt. 5:16.) Paul put the two sides together in his statement: "What we preach is not ourselves, but Jesus Christ as Lord, with ourselves as your servants for Jesus' sake" (II Cor. 4:5). The church first points away from itself to "Jesus Christ as Lord." Nevertheless, it knows that the world, hearing the claim that Christ has brought to the world a life of love that carries with it the power to transform the ways of the world, will turn its eyes to the life of the community. There it should expect to see the evidence of that life: disciples who are "servants for Christ's sake" and a community where the new way is throwing light onto the dark spots of the world's trouble.

In the present race crisis the world should be able to see in the life of the church a community in which all without exception are called to share equally in the family life of God. The world is afraid that the breaking down of old distinctions of caste and color will release forces that will destroy the tenuous safety of our human communities. The church is called to show in its own life that these fears are unjustified and that in Christ there is a way of love that can overcome the conflicts and give true unity. The church is to show the courage that is needed to take the initiative in moving through the old barriers of assumed safety, refusing to allow itself to be limited by the local structures of prejudice. In its life as a city set on a hill it is called to be a "demonstration city," showing the cities of men the promise of their true future as they move toward the city of God.

2. *The church must be like leaven.* (Matt. 13:33; I Cor. 5:6.)

Leaven identifies itself with the lump, but in so doing it slowly changes the character of the whole lump. In like fashion the church is called to work within the world with the leaven of Christ's serving love, looking forward to the time when Christ's love will be all in all, and he will be known as the head of creation.

Here we are introduced to the church's task of working within the institutions of the world to move them toward their fulfillment. In the New Testament, for example, the church is counseled on the way the new life of Christ can penetrate the institution of marriage and the master-slave institution. Slowly that leaven worked within those institutions—undoubtedly far too slowly. But they were changed by the recognition that "in Christ" there is "no male or female" so that a marriage structure that keeps woman in an inferiority situation has not reached its true form; and that "in Christ" there is "no slave or free" so that an economic order that dehumanizes the masses by making them economic machines to serve the comfort of the few is not the institution that God intends for the meeting of the needs of all.

Two points need to be made here:

a. The church all too often becomes so concerned with its own life that it forgets its task to leaven the other institutions of the world.

b. The calling to be leaven is one that changes as the institutional forms alter their shape. The church did have a considerable leavening effect on the life of the family in the old rural world. But now in our urban society the family has undergone considerable changes so that a new task confronts the church if it is to work as leaven to bring this emerging institutional form of the family under the Spirit of Christ.

Take another example. The residence communities of city, suburb, town, village, are undergoing continuing changes in our time. The emerging structures deeply reflect group prejudices and ethnic conflicts. How can the church work as leaven to change the resident community patterns so that they reflect mutual care in the human community instead of protection of political power and economic and cultural privilege?

A further major feature of contemporary society is that large segments of our behavior are routinized. There is a positive side to this. If we were not relieved of the necessity for making many of our behavior decisions, life would become unbearable. But the pattern of routinization creates a powerful tendency for the choice of human wants to be made, not by the conscious decision of the people, but by factors such as the internal logic of the producing mechanisms supported by modern advertising methods.

The question is, How should and can the institutions be subjected to evaluative guidance in this process of routinizing our behavior? If we do not face a closed system of determination controlled by the inner logic of the machines, we must accept responsibility for calling these institutions to their God-given purpose. That requires a clear vision of the purpose of human existence, in short, a theology of hope.

All too often the church has postponed hope to the end

of history and has thereby reduced the institutions to the role of keeper of order until the time of hope arrives. Rather, they must be seen as instruments for reaching out toward God's hope. Jürgen Moltmann has given an effective expression of this.[5] The church is truly "for the world," he affirms, only when it helps the world to reform its structures of hope in the light of Christ's vision of the Kingdom of God.

This has two sides:

a. Because the person is given the promise of reconciliation with God through the forgiveness of sins, this offers him freedom from false hopes and freedom for the purpose of Christ.

b. Because the hope Christ offers is for the world it must be translated into the processes of history. We are offered freedom "for the hope of justice, the humanizing of man, the socializing of humanity, peace for all creation."

This hope must appear today within the institutions where new "wants" are being created and routinized. These hopes of men must be brought into relation to the hope of Christ.

The state religion of medieval times had postponed hope to the end of history. Instead of the church witnessing to a hope that transforms the life of the institutions, it had been given the task of being the center of a divinely guaranteed stability. The Reformers began to break through that limitation in their insistence that the laity are called to serve God's purpose within the orders. But it was only among the left-wing Reformers that a conservative view of this role was overcome. The church generally limited its teaching to the conservative view that the orders are there to keep back the destructive powers of sin. Hope for the world was postponed until Christ's return.

Now that men have growing expectations for the transformation of life, our theology of hope must be related to this new situation. Hope must be translated into the context of our life within the institutions of the world, and related to the hope-meeting capacities of these institutions.

3. *The church must be like salt.* (Matt. 5:13.)

The image of leaven points to the task of transforming the world's structures from within. It is the symbol of newness, of change. The image of salt points to the task of preserving the structures so that they are able to perform their God-given functions. It is the symbol of preservation. Salt keeps the nature of the thing to which it is added. It saves it from decay; it brings out its true flavor.

The church is called to work as salt within the institutions so that they can serve God's purpose by keeping order, peace, justice, health, and by using all their possibilities for enhancing human existence. By preserving institutions from decay they are enabled to fulfill their positive roles; by bringing out their true flavor it better enables them to satisfy the hungers and need of those they serve.

In the past when the Roman Catholic Church undertook to train its members for government departments, labor unions, and voluntary organizations, the Protestants often objected and refused to become directly involved. There was probably a valid intuition here, as well as a serious error. The intuition was that the church was trying to return to its Christendom role of controlling these institutions. Instead of keeping to its role of being salt, the church was subject to the temptation that Christ resisted: the temptation to take over the power of these institutions and to use it for its own interests. The error was to react against that temptation by refusing to accept the responsibility to be salt, working within these institu-

K

tions to help them to serve their own purpose. The task, then, is to train the members to work as servants within these institutions, working alongside their fellowmen in the common tasks the institutions are appointed to serve.

"ECCLESIA SEMPER REFORMANDA"

The Reformers developed the slogan *Ecclesia semper reformanda* as a reminder that if the church is to continue to be the church, it must be subject to continuing reform. This is true not just because of the constant tendency for the members to fall into disobedience and for those in office to turn the church to serve their own desire for status and power instead of directing it to its servant tasks in the world. Constant reform is needed also because Christ is the Living Lord who is restlessly moving on and working within the changing shapes of human hope and need. Yesterday's structures of obedience are today's barriers to new obedience. Obedience is an ever-new event, not a changeless order of continuity.

Hans Küng has explored the meaning of this phrase for the church today.[6] His basic point is as follows:

It is not only because there are mistaken developments and mistaken attitudes in the Church that she has this task. Even if there were none (there always will be) the Church would still have the great task of renewal. . . . The Church . . . is in the stream of time: she has to keep adopting new forms, new embodiments. She has to keep giving herself a new form, a new shape in history; she is never simply finished and complete. She must go into all the world and preach the good news to every creature (Mark 16:15), to all nations, to all cultures, to all ages, until Christ comes again. Such is her incomparably happy mission. Hence she is forever faced afresh with the task of renewing herself. Hence, again, this renewal is not just something which she stringently *must* do, but which she joyously *may* do; a joyful service to the Kingdom of God, looking toward him who will make *all* things new, a new heaven and a new earth.[7]

From that perspective Küng speaks of the failure of Rome to respond creatively to the challenge of Luther. It refused to think out its obedience afresh in this new situation which Luther was facing. And the reason was that it misconceived Christ's relation to tradition. It saw the answers of Christ in fixed form, as law, letter. And when faced with difficulties on the church-world frontier, instead of being open for the need for *renewal* in the church through relating the tradition to the new forms of human life and need, the church responded by the demand of *restoration* and the call for submission to traditional practice.

The restorationist mood that dominated the Council of Trent remained dominant through Pius IX's "Syllabus of Modern Errors," with its rejection of the spirit of modern culture, and through the Vatican Council of 1870. But finally the tide turned and in John XXIII and the Second Vatican Council the church began to move in the direction of renewal.

But Küng then asks: Is it possible that we will now see a moment of supreme irony; that just when Rome is converted to the truth of the Reformers' *Ecclesia semper reformanda,* the Protestants will fall into the error of assuming that their life has been reformed and so become restorationists? Or will we now see together that we need mutual renewal so that we can be free for our ministry in the world?

The Old Testament theme of "the remnant" has crucial significance here. Israel never ceases to be "God's people," but she sometimes ceases to be his faithful people and so becomes subject to God's judgment. This can lead to radical institutional judgment such as the division between the two kingdoms, or the exile in Babylon, or the split between Jews and Christians. But even in the periods of continuity, it is often only a remnant—a small group—that keeps a vital faith alive. The majority "bow the knee to Baal" by allowing their life to become indistinguishable from the surrounding culture.

If the nature of the church institution is such that the majority is constantly falling back into the culture of the day while retaining a formal (and even a "sincere") attachment to the church's doctrine and cultus, there is an obvious dilemma. How can the institution be continually reformed (*semper reformanda*) when only a small minority is truly alive to the faith and free for the mission of Christ in the world?

We see here the reason why it is so often said that the church cannot be a democracy. In one sense that is true. The ultimate rule in the church must not be in the vote of men but in Christ the only truly faithful one. But in that same sense the church cannot be a monarchy, an aristocracy, or any other political model. There is no evidence that hierarchical forms escape the problem of the lapse into faithlessness any better than democratic ones. Bishops, theologians, bureaucrats, may be put in the place of authority rather than "the people," but they are not exempted from falling back into the ways of the world.

Does this mean that we cannot expect institutions to be renewed through their own forms? Does it mean that we can only wait for the Spirit to raise up charismatic leaders or minority movements from within the remnant?

In one sense the answer is yes. But there are "conditions" for reformation for which institutional responsibility can be accepted.

1. We are responsible to put ourselves in the position to hear the renewing Word, since subjection to the rule of Christ is the meaning of renewal. The church tried to put itself under the given Word by creating the canon of Scrip-

ture, the creeds, and the confessions. But it is essential that these be seen in historical perspective. When Scripture, creed, confession, or cultic form are given a timeless expression they no longer draw us into the struggle with Christ in his contemporary battle for man. When these "symbols" of Christ's claim upon us are lifted outside history, they lift the church above history. There is no reformation there. These symbols are vital only when they are struggled with by those who are waiting for Christ to speak to us in the present and as he draws us into his struggle for the future.

2. A second type of "condition" comes from the givenness of human institutions. We know that a coherent minority with a strong vision can have an inordinate effect on the life of an institution in which the majority live in comparative aimlessness. There is a political responsibility for that minority to turn its vision into an ordered program. To wait for the Spirit without accepting organizational responsibility is a theological failure. It is "Docetism"—a failure to see that word must become flesh and idea institution before the saving life becomes incarnate.

Of course, this minority might not be the saving remnant; it may be a demonic pretender. The struggle to turn vision into program must be subjected to the judgment of the word. For that reason, not only is the place of Scripture, creed, and cultus justified, but also the ordered place of teachers with responsibility for the story and pastors with responsibility for reminding the whole body of its dependence on Christ as the true center of its life.

As we wait for Christ to speak the renewing word, we wait in the restless confidence that his word is not powerless. In judgment and mercy, his moment will come. We are responsible for the conditions; he is responsible for the event.

Chapter VIII

The Structures of the Church

It has been a constant theme in this book that the church must join the movement from the world of order, in which it is assumed that society is framed within permanent God-given structures, to the world of organization, in which structures are drawn fully into the changing stream of time.[1]

It has also been stressed that with all the freedom for institutional change that this entails, there is also a necessary continuity in the life of the church. The immersion of the church in history is controlled by the church's story—the story of God's revelation within history of the meaning of all history. This story makes the claim that there is a recognizable shape to God's presence and that the church is called to give a continuous representation of this shape of God's action within the changing forms of human hope and need.

The secret to the faithful discovery of the structural forms of obedience lies then in a radical institutional freedom combined with a radical faithfulness to the apostolic shape of the Chrstian life and mission.

The issue of how the church is to be restructured is urgent here in the United States, not just because the contrast between a modernizing world and a change-resistant church is increasingly incongruous, but also because the conversations between a large group of the churches have reached the point where this question has taken on practical urgency. The churches in the Consultation on Church Union (COCU) have concluded, rather uneasily, that radical restructuring is required. But their question is, On what basis should the decisions concerning these changes be reached? If we can no longer take the simple approach of order by beginning with the changeless marks of the church, this would seem to mean that theology must examine the present structural needs of the church not only in the light of the church's past structures (Scripture and tradition) but also in the light of the understanding of the structures of contemporary life that the social sciences offer.

Theology, in other words, must relate the continuing shape of Christ's presence and of the church's service to Christ to the changing shapes of our daily life. Since those shapes of our life are highly complex, the task can be fulfilled responsibly only when we avail ourselves of the skills of the trained social observers.

It is this recognition that lies behind the work of the World Council of Churches' Study Commission on "The Missionary Structure of the Congregation." This chapter will attempt to draw out of that commission's work a picture of the attitude that is needed as we work toward the necessary restructuring of the life of the church for its mission.

The Call for a Pluriform Church Structure

The working groups engaged in the study were forced to give considerable attention to the meaning of the radical changes in social structure that have accompanied the rise of our urban-industrial society. This forced upon the participants a reexamination of assumptions about the church which most of them had taken for granted. A quote from the report of the North American Working Group will indicate the decisive significance of this. It speaks of the way in which "our unexamined assumptions about a normative congregational form were brought to the surface and made questionable." And it continues:

Now we were open to hear what some of the sociologists were saying to us about the contemporary world: that we are now in a society of multiplicity in which no single structure has a normative significance. It is a world which is a conglomeration of different worlds—home, work, leisure, politics, peer group, etc. So we began to ask whether the church would have to move from its single-form norm to a multiple-structure situation.[2]

This recognition led to a variety of assessments as to the strategy this will require. Gibson Winter, for example, stated firmly: "Residential centers will have to be secondary. . . . Public ministries are prior in our world."[3] Others insisted that this assessment is too strong and that a strategy of presence in the world of the family will still have a certain priority the church must protect. But there was real agreement that any effective strategy requires a pluriform of presence in the variety of worlds.

"Missionary structures," (the North American Working Group) report says, "cannot claim any sacred validity."[4] The structures are *worldly,* in the sense that the church throughout its history has rightly adopted the patterns of common life provided by the surrounding culture as it carried out its task of relating the faith to life. This is true of the parish structures which have become so familiar. They have been around so many centuries, they appear to be changeless! But, in fact, these were adopted from the form of local community life that was characteristic of the medieval settlement that followed the Dark Ages. That form of life lasted so long that the church structures that grew up in that rural village world finally took on a sacred appearance. It began to be assumed that they were given by God for all time.

The recognition of the worldly character of church structures does not mean that the church can adopt or discard its structures at will. Changes must be responsible so that the continuity of the mission may not be lost in the midst of arbitrary change. Nevertheless, it does mean that as the world undergoes radical change, as it has in our time, the church must lay aside its old forms and adopt new ones that will better serve God's purpose.

"The structures which are appropriate for the church are shaped by the world for which it lives."[5] Because Christ is carrying out his saving work in the midst of the world, so the church is called to follow him in seeking to reveal the true worldly life in the context of everyday life.

In our day this can only mean that the structure of the church will be characterized by "pluriformity." This is not new. When we enter the world of the Bible we can soon see that God's presence was discerned in multiform ways. Confessions and theological expressions are expressed in a variety of the thought forms Israel encountered. But today's world is increasingly multiform. We live in an amazing variety of interdependent worlds—family, vocation, education, leisure, politics, sport, etc.—and use a wide variety of ways of thinking, feeling, and acting; consequently, there is a need for a variety of forms of Christian presence.

"It can be said that complementary and even contradictory structures might appropriately be present at the same time, because the one gospel can take shape in contradictory structures in the world. For instance, a ministry among powerless welfare recipients on the one hand, and among powerful businessmen on the other, might well be in conflict with one another, or at least in serious tension, before those ministries move toward some kind of reconciliation."[6]

This will mean that we will move (and are moving) from the relatively uniform structures of church life of the past into a rich plurality of forms. But since these forms together must in some way represent the total shape of the ministry of Christ to our age, we need some typologies that can suggest that wholeness in the fluid processes of continuous change. The study suggests one such typology:

1. *Family-type structure:* In this structure all the members function as one family. Its main task is nurture of its members of all ages so that they may participate in God's mission in the world. Usually residential in character, the family-type structure serves a particular segment of God's world in which it is located. Such a structure needs to be small enough so that solidarity in the service of the larger community is possible among those who feel called into a family of mutual trust. Most present-day residential congregations are not family-type structures although they claim to minister to families. The purpose of their structures needs to be defined much more clearly so that solidarity between members can grow around specific purposes. An example of family-type structure is a small house church in a residential area or in a housing development.

2. *Permanent availability structure:* This structure is basically oriented around long-term tasks and seeks to make services available to people whenever and however they need them without necessarily trying to involve them. An example of

such a structure would be a cathedral or a community service established by the church.

3. *Permanent community structure:* This structure is made up of a group of people who have agreed to live together under a common discipline as an expression of their commitment to Jesus Christ. Examples are orders such as the Taize Community or centers of reflection and formation such as the Evangelical Academies.

4. *Task force structure:* This structure is formed in response to a particular issue or function, and goes out of existence when that issue has found general recognition or when the function is assumed elsewhere. Task forces can be started by any of the three other structures or can come into existence independently as *ad hoc* structures for a particular assignment. In the field of civil rights, for instance, such task forces have come into existence for the purpose of fighting segregation in education and housing.[7]

What does this mean for the present residential congregations? Many of them are multistructured already. But there is need for these to be rethought in terms of the opportunities that are open to them in their particular community. There is such great variety between the communities where the local churches are placed that no single form will do. Planning is needed which helps each congregation to discern the variety of "worlds" to which it can minister at the point of its particular placement. As they seek to undertake this planning, congregations can ask, for example:

What access do we have to such public worlds as government, business, vocations, community action groups?

What are the decision-making processes that intersect with the lives of our members?

What are our points of identification with the powerless groups in society such as the old, the sick, the poor, the discriminated-against?

How much can we meet these various needs through present structures? How can we reshape our life to relate to them? Can task force structures help?

Beyond the present residential congregations, what is required? It is characteristic of our time that many worlds have separated from the world of residence and have become worlds of their own. It is inevitable, therefore, that new "congregations" are forming in these worlds. These new forms are not only in special worlds such as education, leisure, politics, and the rest. They are also related to key issues and movements of our time, such as the struggles for justice, the struggle to relate the scientific and technological developments to meaningful human development, the struggle to develop meaningful centers of human habitation in the midst of urbanization, and the struggle to achieve international peace and order.

PRESENT MOVEMENTS TOWARD A PLURIFORM STRUCTURE

In case it should be felt that these suggestions about a pluriform structure are too detached from reality to be useful and that the vast investment of the churches in the parish congregation (both institutionally and emotionally) means that for many years to come this must be the predominant and basic form, with approaches to the public worlds reaching out from there in task force form, it is important to recognize that rapid developments toward pluriformity are already occurring.

Take, for example, these forms (the list could be increased greatly):

1. A wide variety of *new forms* detached from residential congregations is already developing in the public worlds and the number is growing rapidly:

ministries in metropolitan structures—such as Metropolitan Associates of Philadelphia (MAP), and the Goals Project in Los Angeles;[8]

ministries in the worlds of industry, health, education, leisure, etc.;

ministries in shopping centers;

ministries in movements such as civil rights, antipoverty, the quest for peace;

ministries seeking to train clergy and laity together for participation in the crucial issues of metropolitan life, such as Metropolitan Urban Service Training Facility in New York (MUST).[9]

These new forms are of widely different types and with varying "mixes" of "kerygma, koinonia, diakonia." But their common characteristic is that they are missionary forms seeking to penetrate the worlds beyond residence in witness to Christ the Lord of the church and the world. Any "structure of the church," therefore, which is answerable to present realities needs to see these forms as integral to the total strategy of the church's missionary presence in contemporary society.

2. A less noticed (or perhaps less analyzed) development has been the transformation taking place in the *boards and agencies* of the church in response to these changes in the form of our society. The result is that they have now outgrown the conceptual molds that have been used to describe them.

A quote from the North American Working Group report will set the stage here:

Most of the denominational boards and agencies achieved their present forms in the period when society began its major move from the village to the city. Their purpose then was to serve as the adjunct to the local church to help it deal with some of the new problems of social and personal dislocation.

Hence the saying; "Boards and Agencies exist to help the congregation." So the myth developed that the real "church" is in the local residential congregation. Boards and Agencies are not themselves "church" (e.g., they are not responsible for preaching the word and administering the sacraments), but exist primarily to help the church (local congregations) be the church.

But as the move from village to city culture has increased in speed and as more and more functions of life have separated from residence, Boards and Agencies have taken on more functions that are quite distinct from the work of the residential congregations. But the myth still survives, and it stands in the way of the freedom to develop the forms of church presence now needed in our pluriform society.

It is very possible, moreover, that because the myth obscured the real nature of the development of Boards and Agencies, these institutions have gone through a period of haphazard growth. Now, with the rise of urban-industrial society, the developed forms of these institutions are inappropriate to the tasks of Christian presence that now need to be fulfilled. In any case the myth causes very serious problems: the residential congregations resent the great cost of the Boards and Agencies which are supposed to be purely helpmates to them, and the myth hinders the church exploring the inter-related variety of forms of church life that are now needed.[10]

Those who are familiar with agencies for "home missions," "evangelism," "social action," will recognize the tension. The boards have had to give increasing attention to the needs developing in society outside the world of residence, and the pressures in that direction increase. But are national boards and agencies as presently constituted suitable instruments for ministering to many of those needs? Their own answer increasingly is no, and hence their development of separate agencies (such as urban training centers, regional planning institutes, etc.). Many places and problems now calling for missionary presence are inaccessible both to the residence congregations and to the national boards and agencies.

3. The result of this can be seen in the increasing development at present of metropolitan and regional church structures. For many problems today, residence congregations are too far down the organizational level in society, while national agencies are too far up the line. But too often this necessary development of regional forms is again occurring haphazardly, with inadequate sociological and theological analysis of what ministry should mean at these levels of life.

CHRISTIAN PRESENCE IN THE VARIETY OF NEIGHBORHOODS: SOME IMPLICATIONS FOR THE STRUCTURES OF THE PROPOSED UNITED CHURCH

The conclusion from these (and other) developments in our church life seems clear. We are already far beyond the dual-form suggestion made in the COCU documents, of residence congregation and task force. A pluriform and flexible structure will be needed for the church's missionary strategy today.

Before going on to suggest some lines of approach to be used in developing such a structure, it will be well to recall two familiar World Council of Churches' statements on missionary responsibility in contemporary society. They will set the important theological and sociological framework for what follows.

1. The New Delhi statement on "All in Each Place" sets forth the basic theological meaning of witness which should control our undertaking of structure:

We believe that the unity which is both God's will and his gift to his Church is being made visible as all in each place who are baptized into Jesus Christ and confess him as Lord and Saviour are brought by the Holy Spirit into ONE fully committed fellowship, holding the one apostolic faith, preaching the one Gospel, breaking the one bread, joining in common prayer, and having a corporate life reaching out in witness

and service to all and who at the same time are united with
the whole Christian fellowship in all places and all ages in
such wise that ministry and members are accepted by all, and
that all can act and speak together as occasion requires for
the tasks to which God calls his people.[11]

2. The Commission on World Mission and Evangelism
of the World Council of Churches at its Mexico City meeting in December 1963 took this farther by asking what the
word "place" must mean in contemporary missionary strategy. What are the "neighborhoods" requiring Christians
to gather for Christian witness and service?

"Neighbourhood"—those near us, who therefore have a claim
upon us—must be defined today not simply in terms of residence. In our mobile world lives impinge upon each other
in an increasing variety of "worlds." Thus, for example, in
modern cities and suburbs our lives often are intertwined less
with those who reside near us than with those who are "given"
to us in other communities such as work or recreation or
politics.

The variety and mobility of these increasingly important
non-residential neighbourhoods gives new dimensions to the
task of Christian witness. It suggests the need for new forms of
congregation. It underlines the need to discover the essential
unity of the mission of the Church in relation to the mobile
variety of modern communities. It daily makes more absurd
our denominational divisions which cut across the unity men
are given in these natural communities.[12]

Here then are the general considerations that must lie
behind a decision about "The Structures of the Church."
But how can this be translated into the relatively stable
structure that the church needs at a given moment?

Some General Guidelines

Several general guidelines would seem to follow from
what has been said:

1. The structure needs to be described so that there is *openness to change*—a fundamental characteristic of modern life which the church as institution must share with the institutions of the world.[13] In discussing church structure, however, it is essential to affirm that the church is not simply responsive to the changing shapes of the world. The church's structure must express not only servant presence in the structures of the world but also the converting and renewing claims of Christ. So, for example, the church should not simply follow national boundaries, but is called to express the mission of the community of Christ to break through such limitations.

2. The structure needs to have places where decisions are made concerning the strategy of mission. The description of order in a document for a united church should not spell out in detail the variety of structures for missionary presence, for these will be subject to constant change. But it does need to spell out the way in which decisions will be made in the church through representative bodies that carry responsibility for the structural life of the church. A pattern of accountability is essential so that it is clear who is accountable to whom.[14]

3. The structure needs to take into account the fact that the churches' forms are in process of change from a basically single-form system of the rural past to the multiple-form pattern of the present, and the representation systems that are devised must reflect the realities of what now is as well as the form of what is coming to be.

Places of Planning and Decision

1. The analysis above suggests that a basic unit of church planning and decision-making is needed today that transcends the local scene sufficiently to allow the planning

to relate to the variety of worlds in which we live, but it still must be small enough for manageable planning close to the scenes of action. The suggestion is that this should be *the region* and that the united church should therefore be organized on a regional basis.

To decide how to map the regions is not a simple task. Regions are not just geographical entities. Regions must also be understood in terms of "an area where worlds intersect—such as industry, communications, politics, arts, etc." And since these worlds do not really coincide, the mapping of regions has to be a process that seeks to balance several factors such as:

—administrative criterion—an area that is administratively manageable;

—sociological criterion—an area in which the concentration of decision-making processes, need constellations, etc., is taken into account;

—mission criterion—concern for the intensity of the life-determining issues being faced in the area.

The question of *representation* to the basic regional planning unit is of vital importance. The multiple-mission form within the region must be taken into account. Parish congregations will be represented, but so also will the other mission forms.

A further question in representation is that of the relation between *clergy and laity*. In the relatively simple rural society, when the parish congregation was the norm, the common practice of clergy and laity in equal numbers served the cause of representation well. But now it is not just that the multiple forms of society are calling for different kinds of congregation, and therefore for a principle of representation that takes the variety of ministries into account. It is also true that old distinctions between clergy and lay are in the process of change. What is needed is representation of the missionary involvements in the world.

Although the basic planning and decision-making unit is the region, there are essential forms of involvement in the world both "below" the region in the local communities of residence and "above" it on the national and international levels. As well, there are worlds that do not fit in this vertical geographical hierarchy—functional worlds such as business, communications, education, etc., which will require specialized forms of missionary presence.

2. We turn first to the vital *local communities of residence*. While the region will now become the basic planning unit in our mobile pluralistic society, there is still a sense in which the local residence community must be the basic unit for the church. It is here that the church meets the family. It is here that the largest usable amount of personal time is available for gathering and for training in basic Christian discipleship. What is desperately needed is a way (or ways) for developing viable models of common life and mission in local communities which will take into account the major changes in the nature of communities of residence that have taken place since the inherited local church model was developed.

Such plans are now emerging. A book by Stephen Rose provides a proposal spelled out in practical detail.[15] Other models are available,[16] and ways to a renewal of local church life seem to be opening up.

3. In the *functional or public worlds* of industry, leisure, education, etc., there are already important developments toward discovering the forms of missionary presence that are needed. But so far they are largely haphazard. Basic planning for the actual missionary tasks will need to be largely centered in the regions, but because these worlds

are not geographically confined, national concern with experimentation and evaluation will be essential.

4. The structures of *national life* have become increasingly important, and call for missionary involvement
through national church structures.

National church structures will be needed to undertake
national planning, review regional boundaries, and undertake common policy matters affecting the total life of the
national church. It would seem likely that there will be
considerable decentralization of some of the functions carried on at present by national boards and agencies. Planning and strategy must be kept close to functions—to the
actual places of mission. Hence the importance of regions.
But it must also be said that some important areas of life
function on national levels, and the agencies will be needed
for them.

The principle must be: At each level of the churches'
life that degree of autonomy is needed which will make it
possible to fulfill the missionary task which the structures
of life demand.

5. It is important to remember that there is a further
level of church responsibility *beyond the nation*. And this
is not just a matter of "overseas missions." It is important
that the structure of the united church should witness to
the way in which the gospel points to the transcending of
national boundaries. Although nations are important planning units which the church must take seriously, in another sense the "nation" died at Pentecost, and the church
is called to witness to a community that breaks through
these limits. The structure of the church needs to make
that witness clear—not just by a strong witness in international affairs (though that is desperately needed), but
by concrete structures that break through national limits.[17]

The church is recognizing now the need to break through the structures of ethnic separation as an essential witness to American society. Surely it is equally a life-and-death matter for the church to find imaginative ways of breaking through the structures of national separation as an essential witness to the world.

Laity—The Reference Group for Mission

The traditional clergy-laity image is a simple one from rural life: *a* pastor with *a* flock in *a* community. This is still a good image, but no longer a sufficient one. A World Council of Churches' study on the "Ministry" lists nine or ten "types" of ministry that are present in the church, with the pluriformity of worlds calling forth not only specialist clergy in worlds other than residence but different forms of ministry in these different worlds. The nature of the life that the laity lead in those worlds deeply affects the forms of ministry needed.[18]

Recent Biblical studies such as those of Anthony Hanson on *The Pioneer Ministry* and *The Church of the Servant* have shown how the ministry in the Bible has the task of being the "pioneer" ("model" or "catalyst" to use contemporary images) around whom the wider servant life of the people of God forms.[19] This ministry is sometimes individual, sometimes corporate; sometimes professional, sometimes nonprofessional. Whereas in the village culture the residence congregation clergy were able to be models for the flock in relation to the whole of life, now the residence pastor model is too narrow. The laity see in him a model for the private world, but when they enter their public worlds he is left behind. The clergy are now seeking out ways to go with the flock into these worlds, but it is soon discovered that the ways of being the pastor are very different. Hence the development of ideas of corporate ministries, of mixed professional-nonprofessional ministries.

What is the way forward if this general approach is accepted?

It implies that it is not a sufficient method for a group of churches such as those involved in COCU to proceed along a traditional Faith and Order path to union.

1. As churches struggle along the Faith and Order route it is also necessary that they should go ahead urgently with *experimentation together* in the area of renewing old structures for mission and finding new forms of mission.

Experimentation means action ahead of consensus in order to test out possible forms which can then become agreed-upon forms in the united church. The experiments need to be developed in a variety of areas—local churches, regional models, penetration of public worlds. In this way models can be tested as a way to growing unity-in-mission.

2. Unity and renewal are truly inseparable, and the search for renewal must now be integrated with the search for unity. For this reason we would seem to need something like a Vatican Council through which the presently separated churches can combine the Faith and Order and the experiment-in-renewal routes.

A RENEWAL AND UNITY COUNCIL

Such a council would have as its goal a renewal of the churches for mission, a renewal that includes preparation for that unity-in-mission into which Christ is calling us.

The council would require a rhythm of alternation between joint sessions in which the common concerns of renewal for mission would be developed, and separate sessions in which each member would relate these concerns to present structures and to processes needed to update the churches for mission-in-unity.

Commissions to develop preparatory documents in the substantive areas the council will need to face should include specialists from churches outside the limited group of those involved in negotiating for union, so that the path to renewal and unity that may be opened would be one that would make more easy their later official entrance upon that path.

The time is now ripe for such a council.

1. The renewal ferment now recognizes no denominational boundaries. The concerns welling up across the churches should be seen as the work of the Spirit calling us to recognize the task of renewal not only as a common calling but as a task which we are being called to face together so that God may renew us together as he calls us out of past isolation into the unity of our common mission.

2. So far there has been an incredible surge of mutual discovery across the historic confessional barriers on the Biblical and theological levels. The logic of this is that we must now follow this path of mutual discovery into the institutional channels where the day-to-day missionary tasks of the church are carried out.

3. The time has come for such an encounter. The work of the World Council of Churches in studies such as "The Missionary Structure of the Congregation" and the many experiments that are under way to discover the forms of contemporary mission together are but part of the agenda material that has in fact prepared the way for such a council. The task of the preparatory commissions would be to take such material and order it into a working agenda for the council so that the churches could begin to make the institutional responses that are now required.

4. We face now a time of institutional crisis. The ferment has reached the point where the level of recognition of the need for re-formation (renewal) is now becoming

focused in a question: Can the renewal that God is bringing to his church come about through a planned restructuring of the churches toward the missionary obedience that is now required, or is the inertia and resistance of present structures such that renewal can come only from outside?

5. The very existence of a church union development such as COCU, and the direction it has taken toward affirming that radical renewal is the prerequisite to a true unity-for-mission, has given to many a hope that renewal can also come from within.

What this proposal suggests is that a council for renewal and unity can now seek to correlate the movements for renewal from below with the movement to renewal-in-unity from above.

A council, of course, would not be a cure-all. It would be long and costly. It would create severe tensions and open up deep conflicts. But it is only as we are prepared to pay that cost together that we will be reborn for the mission we are being called to fulfill together.

It has been pointed out that while the Vatican Council was in session a mood in favor of *aggiornamento* was maintained and the process of renovation gathered momentum. When the Council finished, however, the agenda for renewal was returned to the structures inherited from the past and the momentum was slowed markedly. There is a clear lesson here. What is needed is a council that is a continuing process so that the agenda of renewal is kept in the context of expected change. It needs to be clear that a council is not a temporary phenomenon that assumes the business of change for the moment of crisis and then returns the business to the regular church—i.e., the structures inherited from the past. Instead the council as a continuing process must be seen as making it clear that the church needs to be in constant readiness for a planned response to the changing agenda of mission and that it needs a process by which church obedience can be directed to the places where Christian presence is required. Such a responsible process of renewal in our age of constant change is no longer an occasional extra, it must be a continuing responsibility.

The call is to confess that the logic of recent ecclesiastical developments has brought us to the point where the recognized inseparability of the call of God to unity, renewal, and mission demands that the total life of the churches be opened to the renewing winds of the Spirit. Unity will be of little worth without radical renewal at all levels of church life. Renewal will not bear its full fruit unless we are renewed in unity for our one mission.

Notes

Notes

CHAPTER I
THE RADICAL SHIFT IN FOCUS

1. Paul S. Minear, *Images of the Church in the New Testament* (The Westminster Press, 1960).

2. *The Church for Others* (Geneva: World Council of Churches, 1967).

3. *Ibid.*, p. 18, from the "Final Report of the Western European Working Group."

4. *Ibid.*, pp. 69–70, from the "Report of the North American Working Group."

5. Alexander Schmemann, *For the Life of the World* (National Student Christian Federation, 1963).

6. Hans Urs von Balthasar, *A Theology of History* (Sheed & Ward, Inc., 1963). The trend could be illustrated from others: e.g., Karl Rahner, *Mission and Grace* (Sheed & Ward, Inc., 1963); Robert Adolfs, *The Church Is Different* (Harper & Row, Publishers, Inc., 1966).

7. Balthasar, *A Theology of History*, pp. 132 ff.

8. *Ibid.*, p. 144.

9. J. C. Hoekendijk, *The Church Inside Out* (The Westminster Press, 1966), p. 40.

10. Carl Michalson, *Worldly Theology* (Charles Scribner's Sons, 1967), p. 218.

11. I have sought to describe it and to analyze something of its significance in *Faith in a Secular Age* (Harper & Row, Publishers, Inc., 1966).

12. Theologians often refer to this cultural situation as one that places the church in a new "diaspora." We have left our Israel—the culture controlled by the church—and are spread out in a world we do not control.

13. Theologians are beginning to describe ours as an *exodus culture*. Our whole culture is traveling away from its old institutions—leaving all established ways—and is prepared to live in a permanent exodus situation outside the safety of all mental and cultural systems that provide safe structures of order. We live in a situation in which we are moving constantly from one temporary structure to the next.

14. Adolfs, *op. cit.,* p. 3.

15. *Ibid.,* p. 112.

16. Colossians, ch. 3, describes how the new life which the church knows can begin to penetrate the structures of the old world. The church's life is here described functionally even though the language is still "mythical-metaphysical." See *Faith in a Secular Age,* pp. 80 ff.

17. Richard P. McBrien in his book *The Church in the Thought of Bishop John Robinson* (The Westminster Press, 1966), p. 98, summarizes Robinson's statement of this as follows: "The house of God is not the Church but the world, wherein the Church dwells and labours as its servant."

18. *Ibid.,* p. ix.

19. *Ibid.,* p. x.

20. Rahner, *Mission and Grace,* particularly Vol. I, p. 125.

CHAPTER II

THE CHURCH AS EVENT:

THE SERVANT OF GOD'S HAPPENING-IN-THE-WORLD

1. F. J. Leenhardt, *La Sainte Église Universelle* (Neuchâtel, 1948).

2. In *Faith in a Secular Age* I have attempted to draw in the outlines of the picture. But it is important to remind the reader that general agreement on this basic analysis is far broader than the Protestant theological figures used in that treatment. See, e.g., Roman Catholic writers such as Rahner, Congar, and particularly the important series Concilium, published by the Paulist Press.

3. See Paul's exposition of this in Phil., ch. 2, where the church is called to follow the attitude of Christ, who put him-

self at the service of men even to the point of allowing the world to kill him.

4. Walter J. Ong, S.J., *In the Human Grain* (The Macmillan Company, 1967), p. 51.

5. Hans Urs von Balthasar's *Das Herz der Welt* (1945) is not translated. But in English his *A Theology of History* gives a good account of his views.

6. J. A. T. Robinson speaks of Bonhoeffer as the John the Baptist of the world-come-of-age theologies. Certainly his influence has been remarkable, but like most developments in ideas, no one person can be said to be responsible. The idea interprets a profound historical development that had been working its way out from the Hebrew-Christian world view, and through the rise of modern science and philosophy. Bonhoeffer provided us with an effective theological tool for interpreting the significance of the changes.

7. Hans Urs von Balthasar, *Das Schleifung der Bastionen* (1952). Also not translated.

8. An excellent Study Club Edition has been published by Deus Books: *De Ecclesia—The Constitution on the Church of Vatican Council II*. It has a valuable foreword and commentary.

9. In the article "The World in Chains" in *In the Human Grain*, pp. 52–59.

10. *Ibid.*, p. 57.

11. See the discussion of this in *The Church for Others*, particularly the section in the Western European report on "Christian Presence" (pp. 29–35), and the section in the North American report on "Pluriformity of Structures" (pp. 83–86).

12. *International Review of Missions* (World Council of Churches), July, 1966, in the article "Mission in a World of Cities."

Chapter III

The Traditional Views Reexamined: Catholic, Classical Protestant, and Free Church Views

1. In the volume *The Nature of the Church*, ed. by R. Newton Flew (Harper & Brothers, 1952), each major church tradition presented its own ecclesiology. Several commissions were asked to work at the major points of difference between the traditions—ministry, Sacraments, the relation of Scripture and tradition. A good illustration of the attempt to find the

way through the differences to a deeper unity can be seen in the report on "Tradition and Traditions."

2. We should distinguish between church unions within a common ecclesiological family—as when divided Methodists reunite, or when Lutherans of various ethnic groups reunite, or when churches with a common Presbyterian background come together—and church unions where there is unity across major ecclesiological differences. So far there have been very few consummations of this more radical type, although a good many current negotiations are attempting it. It is here that the real issues of the doctrine of the church have to be faced. When the unity of churches within the one family is at stake, important nontheological factors may make the going hard, but it is when union across family lines is attempted that the real doctrinal differences have to be faced.

3. I am aware that Methodists were involved in the union. Methodists in South India (British) could be classified in part with the Congregationalists in their "free church" attitude, but they had retained some of the Catholic attitude of their mother Church of England in their views, e.g., of creeds and Sacraments.

4. COCU at the time of writing has ten negotiating churches: African Methodist Episcopal Church, African Methodist Episcopal Zion Church, Christian Churches (Disciples of Christ), Christian Methodist Episcopal Church, The Evangelical United Brethren Church, The Methodist Church, Presbyterian Church in the U.S., The Protestant Episcopal Church, United Church of Christ, The United Presbyterian Church in the United States of America. They have built on the experience of the Church of South India and of other situations where it was felt the CSI approach had to be modified to allow stronger affirmation of aspects of Catholic tradition on the one side and of left-wing (Baptist) tradition on the other (e.g., Ceylon and North India). In principle they have now come to agreement on all major doctrinal issues and are developing a Basis of Union. But they are emphasizing the event character of the church in their insistence that the form of the uniting church must be radically open to the demands of the situation of mission and the changing moments of obedience. The real interest now is in whether the churches are free enough to risk themselves toward such an open future.

5. Lesslie Newbigin does this in his book *The Household of God* (London: SCM Press, Ltd., 1953). This same approach

lies behind Dr. Blake's suggestion and largely explains the widespread acceptance.

6. A good representative of this kind of ecclesiology is T. F. Torrance. See his two-volume work, which grew largely from the Faith and Order discussions in the first period after Amsterdam, *Conflict and Agreement in the Church* (London: Lutterworth Press, 1959 and 1960).

7. In Chapter IV, I will explore the usefulness of "the Christological analogy" in the church's self-understanding, and will refer to a little of the considerable literature evoked by this development in the Faith and Order story. A typical, direct outcome of this stage is found in the material for the subsequent meeting at Montreal in 1963. See particularly section VI, "Report of the Theological Commission on Christ and the Church," North American Section and European Section, in *Faith and Order Findings*, ed. by Paul S. Minear (London: SCM Press, Ltd., 1963).

8. Gerhard Kittel's *Theological Word-Book* had a tremendous influence on many of the scholars prominent in early Faith and Order studies.

9. So far the post-Bultmannians have not proceeded very far along the ecclesiological study road so it is not possible to draw on that approach to anything like the same extent as that of their Biblical theology predecessors.

10. We have noted already that the Vatican Council document *De Ecclesia* drew the term "people of God" into primacy of place so that the historical character of the church could be affirmed in its pilgrim contingency as over against the ontological fixed view of the church represented in the traditional body of Christ treatments.

11. E.g., the Anglican Alan Richardson in his book *Introduction to the Theology of the New Testament* (London: SCM Press, Ltd., 1958), p. 320.

Chapter IV
A Dogmatic Approach—The Christological Analogy

1. This theme of the church as the sign of corporate humanity is gaining more and more attention in contemporary writing. Just one example from Concilium, Vol. 6, *The Church and the World*, ed. by Johannes B. Metz (Paulist Press, 1965) in the article by Johannes Metz on "Unbelief as a Theological Problem," pp. 71, 73:

M

The believing subject, according to biblical and Christian teaching, is not the individual "I" as such . . . , but the "I" in its original and continuous intersubjectivity, in its *brotherliness*. . . . This supporting ground must be gained ever and again by a loving opening of oneself to others, in a never finished battle against the other alternative of his existence, *i.e.*, refusal of the loving opening of oneself to one's brother and the community. . . . The specifically Christian subject of man's relation to God is not the individual man in his singularity (soul-God). . . . What is most personal in man occurs not in the *privatissimum* of monadic subjectivity, but in love.

2. Emil Brunner, *The Misunderstanding of the Church* (The Westminster Press, 1953).

3. *Ibid.,* p. 17 and p. 107.

4. Eduard Schweizer, *Church Order in the New Testament,* (London: SCM Press, Ltd., 1961).

5. The underlining is mine. The paper is a mimeographed report from the Study Group on the Nature of Unity, July, 1967.

6. Claude Welch, *The Reality of the Church* (Charles Scribner's Sons, 1958), p. 21.

CHAPTER V

THE TIME OF THE CHURCH'S MISSION

1. This is spelled out in Chapter VII, "The Secular Mission of the Church—Service in the Structures of the World."

2. Karl Barth, *Church Dogmatics,* IV/1 (Charles Scribner's Sons, 1956), pp. 83 ff. and 157 ff.

3. Dietrich Bonhoeffer, *Ethics* ed. by Eberhard Bethge (London: SCM Press, Ltd., 1955), p. 73.

4. See, e.g., C. D. Morrison, *The Powers That Be* (London: SCM Press, Ltd., 1956); Ethelbert Stauffer, *Christ and the Caesars,* tr. by K. and R. Gregor Smith (The Westminster Press, 1955); Oscar Cullmann, *State in the New Testament* (Charles Scribner's Sons, 1956).

CHAPTER VI

THE MINISTRY OF THE CHURCH

1. John McKenzie, *Authority in the Church* (Sheed & Ward, Inc., 1966).

2. This aspect is discussed in the next chapter, "The Secular Mission of the Church: Service in the Structures of the World."

3. R. C. Johnson, in an editorial in *Theology Today*, October, 1960, comments on Calvin's attitude on this point: "Calvin assumed, of course, that the mode of government in the Church has been delivered to us in Scripture. It is also clear, however, that he was convinced that in matters of discipline and 'ordering' God had no intention whatever of telling us 'what must be done in each instance.' 'God foresaw,' he (Calvin) comments with remarkable Biblical insight, 'that this would be contingent upon the changing circumstances of the time and that no one form would be adapted to all historical periods.' What we have received in Scripture are 'general patterns' of 'order and propriety.' He says flatly, 'In matters of external discipline and ceremony it was not (God's) will to prescribe in detail.' Rather, this is an integral part of our response to God's act in Jesus Christ."

4. Richardson, *op. cit.*, pp. 312–313. In John Macquarrie, *Principles of Christian Theology* (Charles Scribner's Sons, 1966), essentially the same argument is given. See particularly pp. 368–370, 377–391. I choose these two because they are liberal Anglicans who make full use of historical critical method in their Biblical studies and do not lift "tradition" outside the critical judgment of historians. They are fully involved in the ecumenical dialogue and so approach the material from much the same position as a Roger Mehl. Yet they draw a radically different conclusion from the same "facts."

5. Hans Küng, *Structures of the Church* (London: Burns & Oates, 1965), pp. 136 ff.

6. As a result of his study, Schlier became convinced of the Catholic tradition and joined the Roman Catholic Church.

7. See Küng, *Structures of the Church*, pp. 144 ff., where the evidence is presented for Luther's desire to restore and not to abolish the apostolic order of bishops.

8. The details can be read in *The Basis of Union*, published by the Aldersgate Press, Melbourne, 1963. At this writing, it seems likely that the union will not go through in its present form, but the suggestions here still seem to me to be pointed in the right direction.

9. Jean L. Leuba, *New Testament Pattern* (London: Lutterworth Press, 1953).

10. In Chapter III. In a highly suggestive article on "The Elect People of God in the Service of the World," World Council of Churches, *Bulletin*, Vol. X, No. 2 (Autumn, 1964),

pp. 29–35, R. Martin Achard argues that the break between the Jews and Christians has crucial significance for church union. The real need is for the visible unity of "the people of God." Breaks in continuity were inescapable in God's redeeming process, but restoration at the point of the basic breach holds the key to the others.

11. See an account of this issue in Thomas W. Manson, *The Church's Ministry* (The Westminster Press, 1948); and Karl Rengstorf, *Apostleship* (London: Adam and Charles Black, Ltd., 1952).

12. Rengstorf, *op. cit.*, p. 14.

13. Thomas F. Torrance in *Conflict and Agreement in the Church*, Vol. II, p. 25, speaks of the tension between "horizontal time," ordered in relation to the time of the historical Jesus, and "the vertical time of the Spirit." He comments: "If the church had only horizontal time, then the church would be only a construct of historical succession, having only its temporal origin in Jesus but actually being fettered and determined by its place within the temporal process. Then the church would not be free to have real meeting with the Risen Lord; it would be enslaved to history, enslaved to its own past and all the errors and sins of its past."

14. Published as a mimeographed report in March, 1965, under the title *Ministry*.

15. See Samuel W. Blizzard, "The Minister's Dilemma," printed in *The Church and Its Changing Ministry*, ed. by Robert Clyde Johnson (Office of the General Assembly, The United Presbyterian Church in the U.S.A., 1961).

16. In *Study Encounter*, Vol. III, No. 2 (1967).

17. In Chapter VIII, "The Structures of the Church."

18. Reported in the World Council of Churches' report on *Ministry*.

19. We speak only of "dominance." The parish system that grew up in the Dark Ages as life was ordered into the relatively fixed village system was itself subject to considerable change over the centuries. Throughout the changes, however, there was a central vision of a congregation at the center of the residence community, served by a pastor (or pastors). There were other forms of ministry—in monasteries, education, the military—but the residence congregation was considered the basic church form. That was as it should be, for life was centered on residence. And it is because our society is marked by the rise of a variety of public worlds separated from residence that this single model ministry is now passing.

20. Karl Rahner, *Theology for Renewal* (Sheed & Ward, Inc., 1965).

21. *Ibid.*, p. 38.

22. *Ibid.*, pp. 40–41.

23. *Ibid.*, p. 81.

CHAPTER VII
THE SECULAR MISSION OF THE CHURCH: SERVICE IN THE STRUCTURES OF THE WORLD

1. In Europe there has been considerable discussion of the need to relate mission to the *zone humaine,* an area sufficiently small to allow for a planned ministry, but sufficiently large to include the points of interaction between the major variety of worlds in which its inhabitants live. See the report of the Western European Working Group in *The Church for Others.*

2. Edward Duff, *The Social Thought of the World Council of Churches* (London: Longmans, Green & Co., Inc., 1956).

3. Bonhoeffer, *op. cit.,* p. 177.

4. *Ibid.,* pp. 177–178.

5. Jürgen Moltmann, *Theology of Hope on the Ground and the Implications of a Christian Eschatology* (London: SCM Press, Ltd., 1967).

6. Hans Küng, *The Council, Reform and Reunion* (Doubleday & Company, Inc., 1965), particularly his chapter, "The Permanent Necessity of Renewal in the Church."

7. *Ibid.,* pp. 44–45.

CHAPTER VIII
THE STRUCTURES OF THE CHURCH

1. An important description of the meaning of this change is given by D. von Oppen in his article "Man in the Open Situation," in *Translating Theology Into the Modern Age,* Vol. 2, ed. by Robert W. Funk and Gerhard Ebeling (Harper Torchbooks, 1965), pp. 130–158.

2. *The Church for Others,* p. 62.

3. Gibson Winter, *The New Creation as Metropolis* (The Macmillan Company, 1963), p. 125.

4. *The Church for Others,* p. 70.

5. *Ibid.*

6. *Ibid.,* pp. 83–84.

7. *Ibid.,* pp. 84–85.

8. *Ibid.,* p. 63.

9. *Ibid.*

10. *Ibid.,* p. 99.

11. "The Report of the Section on Unity," *New Delhi Speaks,* ed. by W. A. Visser 't Hooft (Association Press, 1962).

12. "The Message of the Commission on World Mission and Evangelism of the World Council of Churches," *The Ecumenical Review,* Vol. XVI, No. 3 (April, 1964), p. 315.

13. Von Oppen's work on the change from "order" to "organization" as a major mark of the secular world in which we now live has already been mentioned. The significance of this for the structures of the church is considerable. I have discussed this in *Faith in a Secular Age,* pp. 67–69.

14. In modern institutional theory and practice ways are now being explored whereby patterns of interdependence can be developed within institutions (as well as between them). Interdependence means that there are clear, interrelated authority definitions at a given time, but that the relationship of authority between the components in the institution is open to change as the relationship of functions within the system changes.

15. Stephen Rose, *The Grass Roots Church: A Manifesto for Protestant Renewal* (Holt, Rinehart and Winston, Inc., 1967).

16. See, for example, the ecumenical proposal for the new city at Columbia, Maryland, developed by the National Council of Churches and now being implemented.

17. In the proposed Basis of Union for the Congregational, Methodist, and Presbyterian Churches in Australia, there is a Concordat with the Church of South India and a plan for an interchange of ministers, joint training, joint mission board, to make it clear that the mission of the church breaks through the powerful cultural, social, and racial limits the national boundary of Australia imposes.

18. This is discussed in *The Church for Others,* pp. 80–83, in the section entitled "Laity—The Reference Group for Mission."

19. Anthony Hanson, *The Pioneer Ministry* (The Westminster Press, 1961), and *The Church of the Servant* (Alec R. Allenson, Inc., 1962).

Index

Index